A BOOK OF WELSH BIRTHPLACES

Compiled by
JOHN MAY

SWANSEA
CHRISTOPHER DAVIES
– 2002 –

Published in 2002 by
Christopher Davies (Publishers) Ltd.
P.O. Box 403, Swansea, SA1 4YF

A CIP catalogue record for this book is
available from the British Library.

ISBN 0 7154 0739 2

Printed and bound in Wales by
Dinefwr Press Ltd.
Rawlings Road, Llandybie
Carmarthenshire, SA18 3YD

For my wife Lesley
whose concept this was and
who volunteered me to do
the necessary work

Contents

Acknowledgements

It would have been impossible for me to have compiled this gazetteer had I not been able to consult the reference books listed below and I must acknowledge gratefully my debt to these publications:

The Dictionary of Welsh Biography down to 1940 (Honourable Society of Cymmrodorion, London, 1959).

Y Bywgraffiadur Cymreig 1941-1950 (Honourable Society of Cymmrodorion, London 1970).

Y Bywgraffiadur Cymreig 1951-1970 (Honourable Society of Cymmrodorion, London 1997).

The Dictionary of National Biography (1908) and its supplements to 1960 (Oxford University Press).

Who Was Who, Vols. I to IX, 1897-1995 (A. and C. Black, London).

Who's Who of Welsh International Soccer Players by Ian Garland and Gareth Davies (Bridge Books, Wrexham 1991).

Who's Who of Welsh International Rugby Players by John Jenkins, Duncan Pierce and Timothy Auty (Bridge Books, Wrexham 1991).

Pwy yw Pwy, 1981, 1982, 1983 edited by D. Ben Rees and Thomas H. Davies.

Pwy oedd Pwy, 1984, 1985, 1986, 1987, 1988 edited by D. Hywel E. Roberts (both series by Cyhoeddiadau Modern Cymreig Cyf., Lerpwl a Llanddewi Brefi 1982-1989).

The New Companion to the Literature of Wales (second edition), compiled and edited by Meic Stephens (University of Wales Press 1998).

I have also obtained information from newspaper and periodical archives and from general and specialist publications.

My thanks are also due to the many people who kindly replied to my letters inquiring about themselves and others.

JOHN MAY
Tongwynlais, Cardiff

Introduction

Hundreds of places in Wales have produced at least one person who has made his or her mark in Wales itself, in the wider world or in both – artists, actors, industrialists, musicians, novelists, poets, soldiers, sports personalities and others. The vast majority listed have gained their recognition through respectable and praiseworthy, even heroic endeavours. However, there are just a few whose activities have gained them notoriety but here in this wide-ranging compilation they all rub shoulders.

This list of names includes people born in Wales but who are rarely associated with the country. Some examples are T. E. Lawrence (Lawrence of Arabia); the philosopher, mathematician and winner of the Nobel Prize for Literature, Bertrand Russell and the Labour Government's Deputy Prime Minister John Prescott.

In addition to those born in Wales, the book includes people who would never be considered as anything but Welsh but who were in fact born outside Wales. For example, the former Prime Minister David Lloyd George, the actor Windsor Davies and the eminent writer and founder member of Plaid Cymru, Saunders Lewis.

Also listed are a number of people who although born outside Wales and not regarded as Welsh, nevertheless have made important contributions to its cultural, political, social, industrial or sporting life. Examples are the former Prime Minister James Callaghan, Lady Charlotte Guest, translator of the 'Mabinogion', and the second Marquis of Bute, 'the creator of Cardiff'.

The book again confirms the dominance of a very small number of surnames in Wales. Over a half of the 2,100 and more entries are made up of just fifteen names; one quarter by just three – Jones, Williams and Davies.

It is hoped that this book will prove to be a useful reference tool and save trackers of facts a lot of wearisome research.

The larger cities and towns in Wales have a number of distinctive districts which are listed separately in the book as follows:

For CARDIFF also see Gwaelod-y-garth, Llandaff, St Fagans, Tongwynlais.

For NEWPORT also see Bassaleg, Caerleon, Nash, Rogerstone.

For SWANSEA also see Alltwen, Clydach, Cockett, Craigcefnparc, Cwmbwrla, Dunvant, Garnant, Glais, Gorseinon, Gowerton, Kilvey, Landore, Llangyfelach, Llansamlet, Morriston, Mumbles, Oystermouth, Penclawdd, Penllergaer, Trebanos.

For WREXHAM also see Bersham, Brymbo, Erddig, Rhosllanerchrugog.

The larger cities and towns in Wales have a number of distinctive districts which are listed separately in the book as follows:

For CARDIFF also see Gwaelod-y-garth, Llandaff, St Fagans, Tongwynlais.

For NEWPORT also see Bassaleg, Caerleon, Nash, Rogerstone.

For SWANSEA also see Alltwen, Clydach, Cockett, Craigcefnparc, Cwmbwrla, Dunvant, Garnant, Glais, Gorseinon, Gowerton, Kilvey, Landore, Llangyfelach, Llansamlet, Morriston, Mumbles, Oystermouth, Penclawdd, Penllergaer, Trebanos.

For WREXHAM also see Bersham, Brymbo, Erddig, Rhosllanerchrugog.

WALES

A

ABERAERON (Cardiganshire)

David Jones, 1796-1841: Missionary to Madagascar.

Lewis Haydn Lewis, 1903-1985: Poet, winner of National Eisteddfod Crown 1961 and 1968

David Evan Alun Jones, born 1925: Commissioner (Ombudsman) for Local Government in Wales, 1980-1985.

Gareth Price, born 1939: Controller BBC Wales, 1985-1990.

ABERAMAN (Rhondda Cynon Taff)

Charles Butt Stanton, 1873-1946: Miners' leader, Labour and Liberal politician.

Jimmy Michael, 1877-1904: World champion cyclist.

Dennis Williams, 1908-1990: Distinguished neurologist.

Arthur Probert, 1909-1975: Labour MP for Aberdare.

Alf Sherwood, 1923-1990: Welsh international footballer.

ABER-ARTH (Cardiganshire)

John Lewis Williams, 1918-1977: Short story writer.

ABERAVON (Neath – Port Talbot)

John Collins, born 1931: Welsh rugby international.

ABERBARGOED (Caerphilly)

Glyndwr Michael, 1909-1944: 'The man who never was' whose body was used to deceive Germany about the 1944 Normandy landings.

Ralph Griffiths, born 1937: Leading historian.

ABERBEEG (Blaenau Gwent)

George Boots, 1874-1928: Welsh rugby international.

William (Wick) Powell, 1905-1973: Welsh rugby international.

ABERCARN (Caerphilly)

Roy Burnett, born 1926: Welsh rugby international.

Mike Watkins, born 1952: Welsh rugby international.

ABERCRAF (Powys)

Tudor Watkins (Baron Glantawe), 1903-1983: Labour MP for Brecon and Radnor.

ABERCWMBOI (Rhondda Cynon Taff)

Stephen Owen (S.O.) Davies, 1886-1972: Independent-minded Labour MP for Merthyr Tydfil.

Tyrone O'Sullivan, born 1945: Leader of the successful miners' buy-out of Tower Colliery, Hirwaun 1994.

ABERCYNON (Rhondda Cynon Taff)

George Ewart Evans, 1909-1988: Pioneer oral historian.

Tim Cray, born 1961: Folk musician, member of 'Rose Among Thorns' band.

ABERDARE (Rhondda Cynon Taff)

Gwilym Williams, 1839-1906: Judge, landowner and eisteddfodwr.

H. A. Bruce (Lord Aberdare), 1815-1895: Liberal MP: first Chancellor of University of Wales.

David Alfred Thomas (Lord Rhondda), 1856-1918: Leading coalowner.

Ifano Jones, 1865-1955: Poet, author and journalist.

Jack Sheen 1867-1943: Champion professional cyclist.

Sir David Llewellyn, 1879-1940: Coalowner and benefactor of University College, Cardiff.

Arthur Horner, 1894-1968: Miners' leader: first Communist President of the South Wales Miners' Federation, 1936.

Ifor Leslie Evans, 1897-1952: Educationist, Principal of University College, Aberystwyth.

Gwendolen Rees, 1906-1994: Distinguished zoologist, first Welsh woman to be elected a Fellow of the Royal Society.

Mansel Davies, 1913-1995: Distinguished physical chemist.

Sir Thomas Williams, 1915-1986: Circuit judge, Labour and Co-operative MP, government minister and public servant.

Sir David Llewellyn, 1916-1992: Journalist and Conservative MP for Cardiff North 1950-1959.

Emrys Jones, born 1920: Leading geographer.

Robert Morgan, born 1921: Poet and painter.

Emlyn Williams, 1921-1995: Miners' leader, President of South Wales miners from 1973.

Sir Alwyn Williams, born 1921: Leading geologist.

Brynley Francis Roberts, born 1931: Librarian of the National Library of Wales, 1985.

Eurfron Gwynne Jones, born 1934: Writer and educational television administrator.

Gwyn Morgan, born 1934: Labour politician and journalist.

Frances Thomas, born 1943: Award-winning children's author.

David Young, born 1967: Welsh rugby international, British Lion 1986 and 2001.

Darren Morris, born 1972: Welsh rugby international and British Lion 2001.

ABERDARON (Gwynedd)

Richard Jones (Dic Aberdaron), 1780-1843: Wandering scholar and linguist.

ABERDOVEY (Gwynedd)

Thomas Francis Roberts, 1860-1919: Classical scholar, Principal of University College, Aberystwyth 1891-1919.

ABERDULAIS (Neath – Port Talbot)

Lyn Howell, 1907-1988: First secretary of the Wales Tourist Board, 1949.

ABEREDW (Powys)

Thomas Jones, 1742-1803: Noted landscape painter.

ABERERCH (Gwynedd)

Thomas Roberts (Llwyn 'Rhudgi), 1765/6-1841: Quaker and radical writer.

John Evans, 1774-1842: Formidable preacher known as 'the Methodist Pope'.

William Ellis Jones (Cawrdaf), 1795-1848: Poet and printer: in 1830 published 'Bardd Neu'r Meudwy Cymreig', sometimes described as the first novel in Welsh.

ABERFAN (Rhondda Cynon Taff)

Fred Evans, 1914-1987: Labour MP for Caerphilly.

ABERFFRAW (Anglesey)

William John Griffith, 1875-1931: Short story writer.

ABERGAVENNY (Monmouthshire)

David Lewis, 1520-1584: First Principal of Jesus College, Oxford University.

David Baker, 1575-1641: Benedictine theologian.

William Wroth, 1576?-1641: Puritan leader.

David Lewis, 1617-1679: A Jesuit who was the last religious martyr in Wales, hanged and disemboweled at Usk.

Thomas Monaghan, 1833-1895: Awarded the Victoria Cross in India, 1858.

Robert German Thomas, 1840-1866: Missionary killed in Korea.

John Williams, 1857-1932: Awarded the Victoria Cross at Rorke's Drift, South Africa 1879.

Sir Frederick Alban, 1882-1965: First Chair Welsh Regional Hospital Board, 1948-59.

Madeline Thomas, 1889-1989: Actress.

Geoffrey Crawshay, 1892-1954: Soldier, founder of noted touring rugby club and leading public servant.

John Edward Barnie, born 1941: Academic and editor.

John Osmond, born 1942: Journalist, author and Director of the Institute of Welsh Affairs.

Malcolm Nash, born 1945: Glamorgan cricketer.

ABERGELE (Conwy)

Beata Brookes, born 1931: Conservative politician, former MEP and public servant.

ABERGWYNGREGYN (Gwynedd)

Robert John Rowlands, 1880-1967: Poet, winner of the National Eisteddfod Chair 1921.

Meirion Roberts, born 1934: Welsh rugby international.

ABERGYNOLWEN (Gwynedd)

Gareth Ioan, born 1961: Folk musician, member of 'Bwchadanas' group.

ABERLLEFENI (Gwynedd)

Rhydderch Jones, 1935-1987: Playwright.

ABERNANT (Carmarthenshire)

James Howell, 1594-1966: Historiographer Royal to Charles II.

James Owen, 1654-1706: Prominent Dissenter and social reformer.

ABER-NANT (Rhondda Cynon Taff)

Teddy Morgan, 1880-1949: Legendary Welsh rugby international.

ABERPERGWM (Neath – Port Talbot)

Maria Jane Williams, 1795-1873: Noted antiquary.

ABER-PORTH (Cardiganshire)

Evan Thomas, 1832-1891: Leading Cardiff shipowner.

ABERSYCHAN (Torfaen)

Roy Jenkins (Lord Jenkins of Hillhead), born 1920: Senior Labour and Liberal Democrat politician: President of the European Commission, 1977-1981: son of Arthur Jenkins (qv).

ABERTILLERY (Blaenau Gwent)

Sir Thomas Allen, 1864-1943: Co-operative movement leader.

4

Sir Guillhaume Myrddin-Evans, 1894-1964: British representative at the International Labour Organisation, Geneva, 1945-1959.

Ness Edwards, 1897-1968: Senior Labour politician: MP for Caerphilly.

Bryn Roberts, 1897-1964: General Secretary National Union of Public Employees, 1934-1962.

Sir Ivor Brace, 1898-1952: Senior colonial judge: son of William Brace (qv).

Nathan Rocyn Jones, 1902-1084: Welsh rugby international, President of the Welsh Rugby Union 1964-1965: son of Sir David Rocyn Jones (qv).

Percy Archibald Thomas Bevan, 1909-1981: Leading electronics engineer and public servant.

Richard Tecwyn Williams, 1909-1979: Distinguished biochemist.

Mervyn Griffiths, born 1909: Leading football referee: in 1953 the first Welshman to referee an English FA Cup Final.

Jeffrey Thomas, 1933-1989: Lawyer and Labour MP.

ABERTRIDWR (Caerphilly)

Sir Trevor Evans, 1902-1981: Distinguished journalist.

Peter Prendergast, born 1946: Noted artist.

ABERTYSSWG (Caerphilly)

Haydn Davies, 1905-1976: Journalist and Labour MP.

Jack Howells, 1913-1990: Film director: winner of 1962 Hollywood Oscar for the Best Short Film, 'Dylan Thomas'.

ABERYSCIR (Powys)

William Rees, 1887-1978: Distinguished historian: first professor of Welsh history University College, Cardiff.

ABERYSTWYTH (Cardiganshire)

John Roberts (Ieuan Gwyllt), 1822-1877: Minister, musician and editor.

John Young Evans, 1865-1941: Leading theologian.

Sir George Roberts, 1870-1954: Vice Principal University College, Aberystwyth, Principal National Library of Wales, 1944-1950, and public servant.

Sir Goronwy Owen, 1881-1963: Conservative politician and public servant.

Elias Henry Jones, 1883-1942: Author and editor.

John Ainsworth-Davis, 1895-1976: Olympic gold medallist, swimming 1920.

Goronwy Rees, 1909-1979: Controversial journalist and academic.

David Elwyn Lloyd Jones,
1920-1991: Senior civil servant.

David Ifon Jones, died 1924:
Communist – the only
Welshman ever given a
state funeral in the then
Soviet Union.

Ronnie Hughes, born 1925:
Jazz trumpeter.

Teleri Bevan, born 1931:
Senior BBC radio producer:
Acting Controller BBC
Wales 1990.

Dafydd Elystan-Morgan
(Lord), born 1932: Circuit
judge and Labour politician.

Herbert Williams, born 1932:
Poet, author and journalist.

Owen Edwards, born 1933:
Controller BBC Wales 1974-
1981: first Controller of S4C
1981-1989.

Dafydd Hughes, born 1936:
Psychiatrist and Plaid
Cymru politician.

Prys Edwards, born 1942:
Architect, former Chair of
Wales Tourist Board and
S4C.

Roger Rees, born 1944: Actor.

Geraint Huw Jenkins, born
1946: Historian.

Dafydd Roberts, born 1956:
Member of 'Ar Log' folk
group.

Bill Morgan, born 1963: Welsh
rugby international.

ADPAR (Cardiganshire)

John Elwyn, 1916-1997:
Noted painter.

ALLTWEN (Swansea)

David James (Gwenallt),
1899-1968: Poet, winner of
the National Eisteddfod
Chair 1926 and 1931.

Rachel Thomas, 1905-1995:
Leading actress.

Thomas Jones, 1910-1972:
Celtic scholar.

Hydwedd Boyer, 1912-1970:
Novelist.

Alan Lewis Jones, born 1957:
Glamorgan cricketer.

AMLWCH (Anglesey)

William Roos, 1808-1878:
Noted portrait painer.

William Williams, 1890-1965:
Awarded the Victoria Cross
for bravery on HMS
'Pargust' 1917.

AMMANFORD
(Carmarthenshire)

Kenneth Vennor Morris,
1879-1937: Novelist.

Rae Jenkins, 1903-1983:
Orchestral conductor.

Mattie Rees, 1903-1989: Pioneer
Welsh language teacher.

Donald Peers, 1910-1973:
Popular singer.

Ken Etheridge, 1911-1981:
Poet and painter.

Idris Evans, 1923-1985: South
Wales organiser for the
National Eisteddfod.

Eric Sutherland, born 1930:
Academic: supervisor of
the historic devolution
referendum of September
1997.

David Rhys Morgan, born 1937: Political scientist.
Dai Davies, born 1948: Welsh football internationl.
Stephen Rees, born 1963: Member of 'Ar Log' folk group.

Huw Rees, born 1966: Fashion designer.
Richard Elis, born 1974: Actor.

B

BAGLAN (Neath – Port Talbot)
David Jones, born 1935: In 1977, the first Welshman to swim the Bristol Channel.

BALA (Gwynedd)
Evan Lloyd, 1734-1776: Satirical writer.
Betsi Cadwaladr (Elizabeth Davies), 1789-1860: Adventurous world traveller.
Thomas Charles Edwards, 1837-1900: Principal, Bala Theological College.
Robert Roberts, 1870-1951: Popular folk singer.
Patricia Llewellyn-Davies (Baroness), 1915-1997: Opposition (Labour) chief whip in House of Lords 1973-4 and 1979-1982.
Robert Hughes Williams, born 1941: Leading physicist.

BANCYFELIN (Carmarthenshire)
Delme Thomas, born 1942: Welsh rugby international, British Lion 1966 and 1968.

BANGOR (Gwynedd)
William Ambrose (Emrys), 1813-1873: Poet, winner of the National Eisteddfod Chair 1863.
William Owen, 1813-1893: Musician.
John Edward Daniel, 1902-1962: Principal Bala-Bangor Independent College, academic and nationalist.
Glyn Roberts, 1904-1962: Historian.
Gwyneth Ceris Jones, 1906-1987: Chief Nursing Officer British Red Cross Society 1962-1970.
Alfred Owen Hughes Jarman, 1911-1998: Welsh language scholar.
Brenda Chamberlain, 1912-1971: Poet and painter.

Sir Huw Wheldon, 1916-1986: Leading television broadcaster and administrator.

Angus McDermid, 1921-1988: Senior BBC foreign correspondent.

George Hywel Guest, born 1924: Noted organist.

Dewi Bebb, born 1938: Welsh rugby international, British Lion 1962 and 1966.

Gwyn Llewellyn, born 1942: Journalist and television reporter.

Gwyn ap Gwilym, born 1950: Poet.

Ben Roberts, born 1950: Actor.

Gwyndaf Roberts, born 1954: Member of 'Ar Log' folk group.

Joey Jones, born 1955: Welsh football international.

Tudur Huws Jones, born 1955: Member of 'Yn y Bar' folk group.

Huw Roberts, born 1957: Member of 'Yn y Bar' folk group.

Tudur Morgan, born 1958: Member of 'Yn y Bar' folk group.

Angharad Tomos, born 1958: Author, winner of the National Eisteddfod Prose Medal 1991 and 1997.

Arthur Emyr, born 1962: Welsh rugby international and sports broadcaster.

Dafydd Ieuan, born 1969: Member of 'Super Furry Animals' band.

Gwyn Hughes Jone, born 1969: Operatic and concert tenor.

Cian Ciaran, born 1976: Member of 'Super Furry Animals' band.

BARGOED (Caerphilly)

Morgan Phillips, 1902-1963: Labour Party General secretary 1944-1962.

Doris Hare, 1905-2000: Leading stage and television actress.

George Fisher, 1909-1970: Dramatist and theatre director.

Emlyn Glyndwr Davies, born 1916: Leading forensic scientist.

John Tripp, 1927-1986: Journalist and poet.

Alun Hoddinott, born 1929: Leading composer and academic.

Rita Jones, born 1937: Commonwealth Games gold medallist, bowls 1986.

Phil Williams, born 1939: AM, senior Plaid Cymru politician.

Robbie Regan, born 1968: Champion bantamweight boxer.

BARMOUTH (Gwynedd)

John Griffith (Y Gohebydd), 1821-1877: Political journalist, educationist and Liberal.

David Roberts (Telynor Mawddwy), 1875-1956: Noted harpist.

Johnny Williams, born 1928: Champion heavyweight boxer.

BARRY (Vale of Glamorgan)

Sir Robert John Webber, 1884-1962: Prominent journalist.

Margaret Lindsay Williams, 1888-1960: Noted painter.

Barnett Janner, 1892-1982: Liberal and Labour politician and Zionist.

Gareth Jones, 1905-1935: 'Western Mail' journalist murdered by bandits in China.

Roger Livsey, 1906-1976: Distinguished stage and screen actor.

Grace Williams, 1906-1977: Leading composer.

Ronnie Boon, born 1909: Welsh rugby international and Glamorgan cricketer.

Glyn Mills Ashton, 1910-1991: Writer and critic.

Gwynfor Evans, born 1912: Plaid Cymru President 1945-1981: the party's first MP in 1996 (Carmarthen).

Sir Arthur Davies, 1913-1990: Head of the World Meteorological Office, Geneva, 1955-1979.

Dai Rees, 1913-1983: Leading golfer, captain of winning Ryder Cup team 1957: Welsh Sports Personality of the Year 1957.

Elfyn John Richards, 1914-1995: Aeronautical engineer.

David Coleman, 1925-1991: Labour MP for Neath.

Derick Tapscott, born 1932: Welsh football international.

Robert Tear, born 1939: Opera and concert tenor.

Peter Stead, born 1943: Historian, author and broadcaster.

Gareth Williams, born 1945: Historian and author.

John Crook, born 1947: Grand National winning jockey 1971.

Stephen Dodd, born 1967: British amateur golf champion, 1989: Welsh Sports Personality of the Year 1989.

BASSALEG (Newport)

Ifor Hael (Ifor ap Llywelyn), 14th century: Generous patron of poets including Dafydd ap Gwilym (qv).

BATTLE (Powys)

David Morgan, 1833-191: Founder of the major Cardiff Department Store.

BEAUMARIS (Anglesey)

Lewis Roberts, 1596-1640: Merchant and early writer on economics.

Richard Llwyd (The Bard of Snowdon), 1752-1835: Poet and antiquary.

BEDDGELERT (Gwynedd)

Rhys Goch Eryri, fl. 1385-1448: Leading poet.

William Jones, 1826?-1903: Geologist and local historian.

Samuel Millar Jones, 1846-1904: Innovative US businessman know as 'Golden Rule' Jones.

BEDLINOG (Merthyr Tydfil)

Gwilym Davies, 1879-1955: Originator of the annual Children of Wales Peace Message 1925.

Cyril Frederick Walters, 1905-1992: First Welsh cricketer to captain England, 1934 v. Australia.

Gareth Williams, born 1954: Welsh rugby international and British Lion 1980.

BEDWAS (Caerphilly)

Beverley Humphreys, born 1948: Opera and concert soprano.

Jeffrey Whitefoot, born 1956: Welsh rugby international.

BEDWELLTY (Blaenau Gwent)

Zephaniah Williams, 1795-1874: Chartist transported to Australia after the Newport Rising 1839.

James James, 1832-1902: Composer of the music of 'Hen Wlad Fy Nhadau'.

BERAIN (Denbighshire)

Catrin of Berain, c. 1500-1591: Known as 'the Mother of Wales' through marriages to four leading north Welshmen.

BERSHAM (Wrexham)

Robert Ellice, fl. 1640s: Royalist soldier.

BETHEL (Cardiganshire)

Edward Prosser Rhys, 1901-1945: Journalist and poet.

BETHEL (Gwynedd)

William John Gruffydd, 1881-1955: Poet, critic and Celtic scholar: winner of National Eisteddfod Crown 1909: last MP (Liberal) for University of Wales 1945-1950.

BETHESDA (Gwynedd)

W. J. Parry, 1842-1929: North Wales quarrymen's leader.

Frederick Llewellyn-Jones, 1866-1941: Liberal MP, educationist and public servant.

Margaret Hughes (Leila Megane), 1891-1960: Popular operatic contralto.

Caradog Prichard, 1904-1980: Poet and novelist, winner of the National Eisteddfod Crown 1927, 1928 and 1929.

Sir Idris Foster, 1911-1984: Celtic scholar.

John Ogwen, born 1944: Actor.

Ann Catrin Evans, born 1967: Artist.

BETHLEHEM (Carmarthenshire)

Keidrych Rhys, 1915-1987: Prominent journalist and editor.

BETTISFIELD (Flintshire)

Edward Morgan, executed 1642: Catholic seminary priest, hanged at Tyburn.

Sir Thomas Hanmer, 1612-1678: Celebrated horticulturalist.

Sir Thomas Hanmer, 1677-1746: Speaker of the House of Commons 1714: nephew of the above.

BETWS CEDEWAIN (Powys)

Lewis Dwnn (Lewys ap Rhys ab Owen), c. 1550-c. 1616: Genealogist and poet.

BETWS-Y-COED (Gwynedd)
Elfyn Llwyd, born 1951: Plaid
Cymru MP for Meirionydd.

BETWS YN RHOS (Conwy)
T. Gwynn Jones, 1871-1949:
Author and critic.

BEULAH (Cardiganshire)
Owen Thomas, 1878-1967:
Leading geologist and
academic.

BLACKMILL (Bridgend)
Glanmor Griffiths, born 1940:
Chairman and Treasurer
Welsh Rugby Union.

BLACKWOOD (Caerphilly)
Gwyn Jones, born 1907:
Icelandic and Welsh scholar.
Alun Pask, 1937-1995: Welsh
rugby international, British
Lion 1962 and 1966.
Mark Bennett, born 1963:
Leading snooker player.
Rickey Edwards, 1966-1995?:
Member of 'Manic Street
Preachers' band.
James Dean Bradfield, born
1969: Member of 'Manic
Street Preachers' band.
Nicky Wire, born 1969:
Member of 'Manic Street
Preachers' band.
Sean Moore, born 1970:
Member of 'Manic Street
Preachers' band.

**BLAENAU FFESTINIOG
(Gwynedd)**
Idwal Jones, 1887-1964:
Journalist, novelist and

historical researcher for
Paramount Pictures,
Hollywood.
Edwin Owen, 1887-1973:
Distinguished physicist
and public servant.
William Morris, 1889-1979:
Poet, winner of the
National Eisteddfod Chair
1934, Archdruid of Wales
1957-1959.
Richard Bryn Williams
(Bryn), 1902-1981: Poet,
winner of the National
Eisteddfod Chair 1964 and
1968, Archdruid of Wales
1975-1978.
Emrys Lewis Roberts, born
1939: Novelist and playwright.
Father Deiniol, born 1950: Senior
priest, Orthodox Church.

BLAENAVON (Torfaen)
Ken Jones, born 1921: Welsh
rugby international and
athletics track star: first
Welsh Sports Personality of
the Year 1954.
Terry Cobner, born 1946: Welsh
rugby international, British
Lion 1977 and rugby
administrator.
John Perkins, born 1954:
Welsh rugby international.

**BLAENCLYDACH
(Rhondda Cynon Taff)**
Rhys Davies, 1901-1978: Short
story writer.
David Jenkins, born 1912:
Librarian National Library
of Wales 1969-1979 and
award-winning author.

11

BLAENCWM (Rhondda Cynon Taff)

John Haydn Davies, 1905-1991: Choral conductor.

Ron Berry, 1920-1997: Novelist and short story writer.

Frank Vickery, born 1951: Popular playwright.

BLAENGARW (Bridgend)

Frank Hodges, 1887-1947: Miners' leader and subsequently businessman.

Alfred Davies, 1897-1951: President South Wales Area of the National Union of Mineworkers 1946-1951.

Selwyn Gummer, 1907-1999: Anglican canon and editor of 'Pulpit Monthly'.

Jeff Young, born 1942: Welsh rugby international, British Lion 1968.

BLAENPENNAL (Cardiganshire)

John Davies, 1882-1937: Socialist and Workers Educational Association organiser in south Wales.

BLAINA (Blaenau Gwent)

Parry Jones, 1891-1963: Leading operatic tenor.

Will Owen, 1901-1981: Labour and Co-operative MP for Morpeth 1954-1970.

David Watkins, born 1942: Welsh rugby international in both codes, British Lion 1966 and rugby administrator.

BODEDERN (Anglesey)

Hugh Owen Thomas, 1834-1891: 'The father of modern orthopaedic surgery'.

BODELWYDDAN (Denbighshire)

Robert Ambrose Jones (Emrys ap Iwan), 1848-1906: Literary critic and author.

BODFUAN (Gwynedd)

Thomas Williams (Tom Nefyn), 1895-1958: Calvinistic minister and evangelist.

BONTNEWYDD (Gwynedd)

Sir William Henry Preece, 1834-1913: Radio pioneer.

BONVILSTON (Vale of Glamorgan)

J. C. Clay, 1898-1913: Leading Glamorgan cricketer.

BORTH (Cardiganshire)

William Jenkyn Jones, 1867-1934: Political scientist and public servant.

BOW STREET (Cardiganshire)

Thomas Ifor Rees, 1890-1977: Diplomat, one-time British ambassador to Bolivia.

BRECON (Powys)

Sir John Price, 1502?-1555: Author of the first printed book in Welsh 1546: Secretary to Council of Wales and the Marches: monastic visitor for the dissolution of the monasteries.

John Lloyd, executed 1679: Catholic priest found guily of treason and hanged, drawn and quartered at Cardiff.

Sarah Siddons, 1755-1831: Leading actress.

Charles Kemble, 1775-1854: Leading actor: brother of Sarah Siddons.

John Lloyd, 1797-1875: Poet and classical scholar.

John Evan Thomas, 1810-1873: Noted sculptor.

Ernest Howard Griffiths, 1851-1932: Distinguished physicist, Principal, University College, Cardiff, Vice Chancellor University of Wales.

Wilfred Seymour de Winton, 1856-1929: Prominent London banker and collector of prized porcelain.

Lionel Lindsay, 1861-1945: Glamorgan Chief Constable for 45 years.

Sir Charles Thomas Davis, 1873-1938: Senior civil servant.

Joseph Jones, 1875-1950: Freechurch leader and educationist.

Dame Olive Anne Wheeler, 1886-1963: Leading educationist.

Gerald James, born 1923: Leading actor.

BRIDGEND

William Morgan, 1750-1833: Actuary, life assurance pioneer.

Walter Coffin, 1784-1864: Pioneer colliery owner in Rhondda Valleys: First Nonconformist MP (Liberal) elected in Wales 1852 (Cardiff Boroughs).

John Thomas (Pencerdd Gwalia), 1826-1913: Harpist and composer.

Thomas Thomas, 1829-1913: Distinguished harpist, brother of the above.

Sir David John Hughes, 1863-1942: Lawyer: Chair Welsh Board of Health 1919-1928.

Sir David Lewis Evans, 1893-1987: Leading archivist.

Sir Godfrey Llewellyn, 1893-1986: Conservative politician and public servant.

Glanville Llewellyn Williams, 1911-1997: Authority on English law.

Sir Morien Morgan, 1912-1978: Aeronautics engineer.

David Rees Rees-Williams (Lord Ogmore), 1903-1976: Labour and Liberal politician, lawyer and public srevant.

Jack Matthews, born 1920: Welsh rugby international, British Lion 1950.

Joseph Anthony Charles Thomas, 1923-1981: Legal academic.

David Thomas, born 1931: Leading geographer.

Garfield Davies, born 1935: General Secretary of the shopworkers' union USDAW.

Peter Karrie, born 1946: Leading man in popular musicals.

David Emanuel, born 1952:
Fashion designer.

Gerald Battrick, 1947-1998:
Leading tennis player.

Wayne David, born 1957:
Labour MEP.

Steve Brace, born 1961:
Marathon runner, winner
of the 1989 Paris Marathon.

Huw Edwards, born 1961:
Radio and television
journalist.

Christopher Rees, born 1965:
Leading Welsh badminton
player.

Robert Howley, born 1970:
Welsh rugby international,
British Lion 1997 and 2001.

Scott Gibbs, born 1971: Welsh
rugby international in both
codes. British Lion 1997
and 2001.

Wayne Proctor, born 1972:
Welsh rugby international.

BRITHDIR (Caerphilly)

Lewis Boddington, 1906-1994:
Inventor of the angled flight
deck on aircraft carriers.

Keith Rowland, born 1936:
Welsh rugby international,
British Lion 1962 and rugby
administrator.

BRITON FERRY (Neath – Port Talbot)

Bussey Mansel, 1623-1699:
Parliamentary soldier.

Emrys Jones, 1911-1989:
Glamorgan cricketer.

Harry Parr-Davies, 1914-1955:
Popular songwriter and
musician.

Ivor Owen Thomas, 1929-1987:
Trade union official, National
Union of Railwaymen and
Labour MP.

Mavis Nicholson, born 1930:
Journalist and broadcaster.

Linda Evans, born 1942:
Commonwealth Games
gold medallist 1986, bowls.

Leighton Phillips, born 1949:
Welsh football international.

David Pickering, born 1960:
Welsh rugby international.

BRYMBO (Wrexham)

Thomas Pryce, 1852-1909:
Labour Prime Minister of
South Australia 1905-1909.

BRYNAMAN (Carmarthenshire)

Thomas Stephens, 1856-1906:
Musician and conductor.

Thomas Isaac Mardy-Jones,
1879-1970: Economist and
socialist politician.

Sir Leslie Jones, 1884-1968:
Leading industrialist.

Bryan Martin Davies, born
1933: Award-winning poet
and Welsh language teacher.

Roy Noble, born 1942: Radio
and television broadcaster.

Dafydd Iwan, born 1943:
Plaid Cymru politician and
singer/songwriter.

BRYNCROES (Gwynedd)

Moses Griffiths, 1747-1819:
Noted painter.

BRYNEGLWYS (Denbighshire)

David Rowland, 1552-1598: Historian and scholar, thought to have been the first graduate of Jesus College, Oxford.

BRYNMAWR (Blaenau Gwent)

Sir Thomas Phillips, 1801-1867: Mayor of Newport during the Chartist Rising 1839: knighted for helping in its suppression.

Sir Bartle Frere, 1815-1884: Colonial administrator in India and South Africa.

David Thomas Lewis, 1909-1992: Distinguished chemist.

BUCKLEY (Flintshire)

Frederick Birks, 1894-1917: Awarded the Victoria Cross posthumously in France.

BUILTH WELLS (Powys)

Hilda Vaughan, 1892-1985: Novelist.

John Hussey Hamilton (Lord Swansea) born 1925: Commonwealth Games rifle shooting gold 1966, silver 1982.

Jeremy Pugh, born 1961: Welsh rugby international.

BURRY PORT (Carmarthenshire)

Linford Llewelyn Rees, born 1914: Leading psychiatrist and father of Angharad Rees.

BUTTINGTON (Powys)

Sir William Boyd Dawkins, 1837-1929: Geologist who discovered the Kent coalfield in 1882.

BWLCHLLAN (Cardiganshire)

George Noakes, born 1924: Archbishop of Wales 1987-1991.

C

CADOXTON-JUXTA-NEATH (Neath – Port Talbot)

David Thomas, 1794-1882: Iron and steel industry pioneer in the USA.

Lady Dorothy Stanley (née Tennant), died 1926: Married Sir Henry Morton Stanley (qv): edited his autobiography.

Sir David Evans Bevan, 1902-1973: Industrialist and public servant.

CAERAU (Rhondda Cynon Taff)

Allan Bateman, born 1956: Welsh rugby international, British Lion 1997.

15

CAERAU (Bridgend)

Sir Rhys Hopkin Morris, 1888-1956: Barrister, Liberal MP, director of BBC Welsh Region 1936-1945.

CAERLEON (Newport)

Lewis of Caerleon, fl.1490s: Physician to Catherine of Aragon.

John Lloyd, c. 1480-1523: Musician and official at Henry VIII's Chapel Royal.

Lewis Evans, 1755-1827: Fellow of the Royal Society and great-grandfather of Sir Arthur Evans, excavator in Crete.

Arthur Machen, 1863-1947: Novelist and translator.

Rhys Watcyn Williams, born 1946: German language scholar.

CAERNARFON (Gwynedd)

Edward II, 1284-1327: First English Prince of Wales, murdered at Berkeley Castle.

Anna Hariette Crawford, 1834-1914: Tutor to the royal children of Siam, 1862-1867.

Lewis Jones, 1836-1905: Pioneer settler in Patagonia: one-time Argentine governor there.

Thomas Llewellyn Thomas, 1840-1897: Scholar and linguist: authority on the Basque language.

Thomas Hudson-Williams, 1873-1961: Classical scholar and educationist.

Lionel Rees, 1884-1955: Awarded the Victoria Cross in France 1916.

Huw Owen Williams (Huw Menai), 1888-1961: Noted poet.

Emrys Owain Roberts, 1910-1990: Poet and Liberal MP for Merioneth 1945-1956: public servant.

Roy Bohana, born 1938: Conductor and adjudicator: founder of Cardiff Polyphonic Choir: Musical Director Llangollen International Musical Eisteddfod.

Gareth Miles, born 1938: Author and playwright.

Winston Roddick, born 1940: Barrister: first Counsel General to Welsh Assembly.

Dafydd Wigley, born 1943: Plaid Cymru AM and MP: former party president.

CAERPHILLY

Evan James, 1800-1878: Composer of the words of 'Hen Wlad fy Nhadau'.

Sir William James Thomas, 1867-1945: Coalowner, philanthropist and public servant.

David Garnet Davey, born 1912: Lead the team which found sleeping sickness cure.

Tommy Cooper, 1922-1984: Comedian and conjuror.

Alan Williams, born 1930: Labour MP for Swansea West.

Michael Voyle, born 1970: Welsh rugby international.

CAERSWS (Powys)

John Morgan Jones, 1903-1989: Agricultural economist.

CAERWEN (Anglesey)
Roger Webster, 1926-1975:
Distinguished educationist.

CAERWYS (Flintshire)
Thomas Jones, 1756-1820:
Hymnwriter and author.
Angharad Llwyd, 1780-1866:
Noted antiquarian.

CALDICOT
(Monmouthshire)
John Edwards (Siôn Treredyn),
1606?-1660: Cleric, translator
and Welsh language
enthusiast.

CAPEL CYNON
(Cardiganshire)
Thomas Jacob Thomas, 1873-
1945: Poet, winner of the
National Eisteddfod Chair
1913.

CAPEL DEWI
(Carmarthenshire)
J. Cynddylan Jones, 1841-
1930: Theologian and
Biblical scholar.
Ieuan Evans, born 1964: Welsh
rugby international, British
Lion 1989, 1993 and 1997.

CAPEL ISAAC
(Carmarthenshire)
William Leslie Richards, 1916-
1989: Poet and novelist.

CARDIFF
Rawlins White, executed
1555: Protestant martyr
burnt at the stake in Cardiff.

Sir Henry Morgan, c. 1635-
1688: Buccaneer, Deputy
Governor of Jamaica 1674.
(His birth here is not certain).
Taliesin Williams, 1787-1847:
Poet, son of Edward Williams
(Iolo Morganwg) (qv).
Robert Shields, 1827-1864:
Awarded the Victoria Cross
in the Crimean War 1856.
Sir Alfred Thomas (Lord
Pontypridd), 1840-1927:
Liberal, prominent
businessman and first
President of the National
Museum of Wales.
Sir Charles Melhuish, 1860-
1943: Lord Mayor of
Cardiff, authority on the
Poor Law.
Clara Novello Davies, 1861-
1943: Conductor of Royal
Welsh Ladies Choir: mother
of Ivor Novello (qv).
Sir William Seager, 1862-1941:
Leading Cardiff shipowner.
Sir Illtyd Thomas, 1864-1943:
Engineer and educationist:
Lord Mayor and Freeman
of Cardiff.
Ormonde Maddock Dalton,
1866-1945: Medieval scholar
and archaeologist.
Selwyn Biggs, 1872-1943:
Welsh rugby international.
Charles Coles, 1879-1947:
First Principal of Cardiff
Technical College.
Sir William Karsant Lewis,
1877-1950: Leading foreign
correspondent.
Nixon Grey (David McNeil),
1880-1952: Music hall star.

George Mackintosh Lindsay, 1880-1956: Major-general, tank warfare expert.

Jim Driscoll, 1881-1925: Champion featherweight boxer.

Sir Thomas Lewis, 1881-1945: Leading physiologist.

Norman Riches, 1883-1975: Glamorgan cricketer, first captain of the county championship side from 1921.

Sir Herbert Merrett, 1886-1959: Leading businessman: Chair of Cardiff City, President of Glamorgan Cricket Club.

Paulo Radmilovich, 1886-1968: Olympic gold medallist in swimming events in 1908, 1912 and 1920.

Ernest Thompson Willows, 1886-1926: Airship pioneer: holder of Royal Aero Club's No.1 airship pilot certificate.

Harry Sherman, 1887-1961: Founder of Shermans Football Pools, philanthropist: brother of Abe (qv).

Bertrand Turnbull, 1887-1943: Glamorgan cricketer.

Leonard Walter Brockereton, 1888-1966: Journalist and barrister: first head of the Canadian Broadcasting Corporation.

David Jacobs, 1888-1976: Olympic track relay gold medallist 1912.

David Prosser, 1889-1974: Editor 'Western Mail'.

Irene Steer, 1889-1977: Olympic gold medallist, swimming 1912.

Frederick Barter, 1891-1953: Awarded the Victoria Cross in France, 1917.

Wickham (Wick) Powell, 1892-1955: Welsh rugby international.

John Elliot Seager, 1892-1955: Leading Cardiff shipowner and public servant.

Edward William Williamson, 1892-1952: Bishop of Swansea and Brecon 1939.

Jack Corsi, 1893-1949: Welsh rugby league international and music hall artist.

Ivor Novello (David Ivor Davies), 1893-1951: Leading composer and stage and screen actor.

Abe Sherman, 1893-1965: Founder of Shermans Football Pools, philanthropist: brother of Harry (qv).

Fred Keenor, 1894-1972: Welsh football international, captain of FA Cup Final winners Cardiff City 1927.

William Henry (Bill) Smith, 1894-1968: First manager Welsh National Opera.

Walter Bishop (Waldini), 1895-1966: Popular South Wales showman and musician.

Lilian Davies, 1895-1932: Leading actress and singer.

Arthur Cornish, 1897-1948: Welsh rugby international.

Kathleen Freeman, 1897-1959: Successful novelist.

Hilary Marquand, 1901-1972: Distinguished economist and Labour MP.

Charles Curran, 1903-1972: Leading journalist.

Lyn Joshua, 1901-1947: Popular broadcaster: joint composer of 'We'll Keep a Welcome'.

R. M. Lockley, 1903-2000: Naturalist and author.

Jim Sullivan, 1903-1977: Welsh rugby league international with a record 60 caps.

Herbert Bowden (Lord Aylestone), 1905-1994: Senior Labour and Liberal Democrat politician: Chair Independent Broadcasting Authority.

Percy Cudlipp, 1905-1962: Leading Fleet Street journalist, brother of Hugh and Reginald (qv).

Hubert Johnson, 1905-1979: Leading Cardiff businessman, President of Cardiff RFC and Llandaff Rowing Club.

Frederick James Wilkins, 1905-1965: Managing director of Glaxo Ltd.

Maurice Turnbull, 1906-1944: Glamorgan cricket captain, son of Bertrand Turnbull (qv).

Harry Bowcott, born 1907: Welsh rugby international, President of the Welsh Rugby Union 1974-1975.

Griffith James Powell, 1907-1999: Leading aviation executive: holder of the trans-Atlantic flight record from 1937-1944.

Hugh (Binkie) Beaumont, 1908-1973: West End theatre impressario.

Reginald Cudlipp, born 1910: Leading journalist: brother of Percy and Hugh (qv).

Merlyn Oliver Evans, 1910-1973: Noted painter.

Alec Templeton, 1910-1963: Jazz pianist.

Maurice Edelman, 1911-1975: Labour MP and novelist.

Jack Peterson, 1911-1990: Champion heavyweight and light heavyweight boxer.

Gus Risman, 1911-1994: Welsh rugby international in both codes.

Hugh Cudlipp (Lord), 1913-1998: Leading journalist, one time Chair of the Mirror group: brother of Percy and Reginald (qv).

José (Joe) Deniz, 1913-1994: Jazz guitarist.

Alun Llywelyn-Williams, 1913-1988: Award-winning poet: critic and editor.

R. S. Thomas, 1913-2000: Award-winning poet.

John George Williams, 1913-1997: Noted environmentalist and author.

Tony Duncan, 1914-1998: Leading amateur golfer.

Tessie O'Shea, 1914-1995: Leading singer and entertainer.

Charles Henry (Pat) Barnett, born 1915: Jazz trumpeter and singer.

Cyril Hodges, 1915-1974: Poet.

Roald Dahl, 1916-1990: Highly successful author, particularly of children's books.

Sir Raymond Gower, 1916-1989: Journalist and Conservative MP for Barry.

Leo Abse, born 1917: Lawyer and Labour MP.

Frank Greenaway, born 1917: Authority on the history of science.

Gwyn Owain Jones, born 1917: Novelist.

Peter Philip, born 1920: Playwright.

Sir Haydn Tudor Evans, born 1920: High Court judge.

Harold Rubens, born 1921: Concert pianist.

Dannie Abse, born 1923: Award-winning poet and author: brother of Leo (qv).

John Marles Eynon, born 1923: Architect and painter.

Jim Pleass, born 1923: Glamorgan cricketer.

Donald Baverstock, 1924-1995: Television producer.

Stewart Williams, born 1925: Local historian, publisher and author.

Hugh David, born 1926: Actor.

Jack Brooks (Lord), born 1927: Labour politician: Chair Welsh Labour Party.

Bernice Rubens, born 1927: Prize-winning novelist.

Stan Stennett, born 1927: Popular comedian and actor.

Bobi Jones, born 1929: Author and critic.

Clem Thomas, 1929-1996: Welsh rugby international, journalist and author.

James Tucker, born 1929: Journalist and novelist.

Edward (Ted) Milward, born 1930: Welsh language scholar.

Brian Morris (Lord), 1930-2001: Author, educationist and public servant.

Sir Bernard Knight, born 1931: Leading pathologist and novelist.

Leon Eagles, born 1932: Actor.

Walter Marshall (Lord), 1932-1996: Distinguished physicist.

Alun Priday, born 1932: Welsh rugby international.

Colin Webster, 1932 -2001: Welsh football international.

Billy Boston, born 1934: Welsh rugby league international.

Joe Erskine, 1934-1990: Champion heavyweight boxer; Welsh Sports Personality of the Year 1956.

Paul Flynn, born 1935: Labour MP for Newport West.

Vincent Kane, born 1935: Radio and television journalist.

Gwilym Roberts, born 1935: Leading Welsh language teacher.

Andrew Davies, born 1936: Award-winning author: television playwright.

Jane Phillips, born 1936: Founder of the Caricature Theatre in Cardiff 1963.

Dame Shirley Bassey, born 1937: International singing star.

Gillian Clarke, born 1937: Award-winning poet.

Prys Morgan, born 1937:
Historian, award-winning
writer.

Sir David Rowe-Beddoe, born
1937: Chair of Welsh
Development Agency 1993.

Richard Marquand, 1938-
1987: Film director.

Gilbert Ruddock, born 1938:
Poet and historian.

Alun Guy, born 1939: Choral
conductor.

Rhodri Morgan, born 1939:
AM and MP Labour for
Cardiff West. First Minister,
National Assembly for
Wales, 2000.

Norman Rees, born 1939:
Television journalist.

David Broome, born 1940:
World show jumping
champion 1961, 1967 and
1969: Olympic medallist,
equestrian bronze 1952, 1960.

Maureen Evans, born 1940:
Popular singer.

Brian Josephson, born 1940:
Physicist, Nobel Prize
winner 1973.

Peter King, 1940-1989:
Novelist and playwright.

John Mantle, born 1942:
Welsh rugby international
in both codes.

Gil Reece, born 1942: Welsh
football international.

Howard Stringer, born 1942:
Senior CBS and Sony
executive in the USA.

John Humphrys, born 1943:
Radio and television
broadcaster.

Bill Raybould, born 1944:
Welsh rugby international.

Peter Rodrigues, born 1944:
Welsh football international.

Eddie Avoth, born 1945:
Champion light heavyweight
and lightweight boxer.

Dave Burns, born 1946: Folk
singer.

Duncan Bush, born 1946: Poet.

Roger Davis, born 1946:
Glamorgan cricketer.

John Mahoney, born 1946:
Welsh football international.

Frank Hennessy, born 1947:
Folk singer and broadcaster.

Peter Finch, born 1947: Poet,
Chief Executive, Welsh
Academy.

David Jenkins, born 1948:
General Secretary Wales TUC.

Michael Barratt (Shakin'
Stevens), born 1948:
Popular singer.

Ken Follett, born 1949: Best-
selling novelist.

Heather Jones, born 1949:
Folk singer.

Angharad Rees, born 1949:
Leading actress.

John Toshack, born 1949:
Welsh football international
and leading club manager:
Welsh Sports Personality of
the Year 1981.

John Turner, born 1949:
Member of 'Rose Among
Thorns' band.

J.P.R. Williams, born 1949:
Welsh rugby international,
British Lion 1971 and 1974.

Martyn Woodroffe, born 1950:
Olympic silver medallist,
swimming 1968: Welsh Sports
Personality of the Year 1968.

Terry Yorath, born 1950: Welsh football international and manager.

Griff Rhys Jones, born 1953: Popular comedy actor and writer.

Derek Morgan, born 1953: Member of 'Rose Among Thorns' band.

Alan Wilkins, born 1953: Glamorgan cricketer and sports broadcaster.

Ian Eidman, born 1957: Welsh rugby international.

Terry Holmes, born 1957: Welsh rugby international, British Lion 1980 and 1983.

Oliver Reynolds, born 1957: Award-winning poet.

Marc Evans, born 1959: Film director.

Elaine Morgan, born 1960: Folk singer.

Jeremy Bowen, born 1962: BBC foreign correspondent.

Sally Moore, born 1962: Artist.

Mark Ring, born 1962: Welsh Rugby international.

Lilio Rolant, born 1962: Member of 'Bwchadanas' folk group.

Glen Webbe, born 1962: Welsh rugby international.

Adrian Hadley, born 1963: Welsh rugby international.

Hugh Morris, born 1963: Glamorgan and England cricketer.

Nigel Walker, born 1963: Welsh rugby international, track athlete and sports broadcaster.

Neil Slatter, born 1964: Welsh football international.

Nicky Piper, born 1966: Champion light heavyweight boxer and television sports presenter.

Huw (Bunf) Bunford, born 1967: Member of 'Super Furry Animals' band.

Colin Jackson, born 1967: Olympic silver medallist, 110 metres hurdles 1988. Welsh Sports Personality of the Year, 1988, 1993 and 1999.

Robert Morgan, born 1967: Commonwealth Games medallist, diving, silver 1986, gold 1990.

Steve Robinson, born 1968: Champion featherweight boxer, Welsh Sports Personality of the Year 1994.

Rhodri Williams, born 1968: Television presenter.

Tanni Grey, born 1969: Paralympics Games medallist, four gold 1992 and 2000, one gold three silver 1996: Welsh Sports Personality of the Year 1992.

Lucy Cohen, born 1969: Television presenter.

Gareth Llywellyn, born 1969: Welsh rugby international.

Cerys Matthews, born 1969: Singer with 'Catatonia' band.

Sarah Loosemore, born 1971: Leading tennis player.

Ryan Giggs, born 1973: Welsh football international; Welsh Sports Personality of the Year 1996.

Jason Stone, born 1973: Leading ice hockey player.

Ioan Gruffudd, born 1974:
Leading film and television
actor.

Barry Jones, born 1974:
Champion super-
featherweight boxer.

Eos Chater, born 1975:
Member of the classical
female quartet Bond.

Matthew Rhys, born 1975:
Successful stage, screen and
television actor.

Guto Pryce, born 1976:
Member of 'Super Furry
Animals' band.

Charlotte Church, born 1986:
Soprano, singing prodigy.

CARDIGAN
(Cardiganshire)

William Gambould, 1672-
1728: Grammarian,
complier of English-Welsh
dictionary.

John Nash, 1752-1835:
Distinguished architect.

Moelwyn Hughes, 1897-1955:
Labour MP for Carmarthen
and Islington.

Roderic Bowen, 1913-2001:
Lawyer and Liberal politician.

David Clay-Jones, 1923-1996:
radio gardening expert.

Brian Morris, born 1930: Poet
and critic.

Brynmor Williams, born 1951:
Welsh rugby international,
British Lion 1977 and
television sports reporter.

Hywel Davies, born 1956:
Grand National winning
jockey 1985.

CARMARTHEN
(Carmarthenshire)

Stephen Hughes, 1622-1688:
Translator and editor.

Bridget Bevan, 1698-1779:
Educationist who financed
the circulating schools of
Griffith Jones (qv).

John Thomas (Ieuan Ddu),
1795-1871: Poet, singer and
conductor: early eisteddfodwr.

Brinley Richards, 1819-1885:
Composer, whose work
included 'God Bless the
Prince of Wales'; friend of
Chopin.

Sir Lewis Morris, 1833-1907:
Poet and critic.

William John Davies, 1891-
1975: Diplomat and Japanese
language authority.

Emrys George Bowen, 1900-
1983: Distinguished
geographer.

Sir Lynn Ungoed-Thomas,
1904-1972: High Court
judge: Labour MP for Barry
and Llandaff.

W. E. (Willie) Jones, born
1916: Glamorgan cricketer.

Mervyn Jones, born 1920:
Grand National winning
jockey 1940.

Sir David Glyndwr Tudor
Williams, born 1930:
Distinguished legal academic.

Denzil Davies, born 1938:
Senior Labour politician.

Geraint Talfan Davies, born
1943: Controller BBC Wales
from 1990.

Derec Llwyd Morgan, born
1943: Poet and critic.

Tony Curtis, born 1946: Poet, first professor of poetry in Wales, University of Glamorgan.

Roy Bergiers, born 1950: Welsh rugby international, British Lion 1974.

Iwan Roberts, born 1953: Member of 'Yn y Bar' folk group.

Mike Doyle, born 1960: Popular comedian.

Angharad Mair, born 1961: Athlete and television presenter.

Robert Dickie, born 1964: Champion super featherweight boxer.

Megan Childs, born 1971: Member of 'Gorky's Zygotic Mynci' band.

Euros Rowlands, born 1971: Member of 'Gorky's Zygotic Mynci' band.

Euros Childs, born 1975: Member of 'Gorky's Zygotic Mynci' band.

Richard James, born 1975: Member of 'Gorky's Zygotic Mynci' band.

John Lawrence, born 1975: Member of 'Gorky's Zygotic Mynci' band.

CARMEL (Gwynedd)

Henry Parry-Williams, 1858-1925: Celtic scholar and poet: father of T. H. Parry-Williams (qv).

David James Davies, 1893-19: Political thinker, nationalist.

Sir Thomas Parry, 1904-1985: Critic and editor: educationist, Principal University College, Aberystwyth.

CARREG-CEFN (Anglesey)

William Owen, born 1935: Dramatist.

CARREGHOFA (Powys)

David Jones, 1941-1994: Noted historian.

CEFNBRYNBRAIN (Carmarthenshire)

Derec Llwyd Morgan, born 1943: Critic and award-winning poet.

CEFNDDWYSARN (Gwynedd)

T. E. Ellis, 1859-1899: Leading Liberal politician.

Robert Lloyd (Llwyd o'r Bryn), 1888-1961: Poet, leading eisteddfod adjudicator.

CEFNEITHEN (Carmarthenshire)

Carwyn James, 1929-1983: Welsh rugby international and leading coach.

Delme Bryn-Jones, 1934-2001: Leading operatic baritone.

Ronnie Williams, 1939-1997: Popular actor and writer.

Gwynoro Jones, born 1942: Labour and Liberal Democrat politician.

Barry John, born 1945: Welsh rugby international, British Lion 1973.

CELLAN (Cardiganshire)

Moses Williams, 1685-1742: Antiquary.

John Thomas, 1838-1905: Photographer: made invaluable studies of people and places in Victorian Wales.

Griffith John Williams, 1892-1963: Eminent literary historian.

CEMAES (Powys)
John Roderick (Siôn Rhydderch), 1673-1735: Lexicographer, publisher of an English-Welsh dictionary 1725.

David Vaughan Davies, 1911-1969: Authority on anatomy, public servant.

CENARTH (Cardiganshire)
Eluned Phillips (Luned Teifi), born 1915: Poet, in 1967 became only the second woman to win a National Eisteddfod Crown.

CERRIG-Y-DRUDION (Conwy)
Edward Morris, 1607-1689: Poet.
Robert Price, 1655-1733: Judge and Tory MP.
John Jones (Jac Glan-y-gors), 1766-1821: Satirical writer, republican and pacifist.

CHEPSTOW (Monmouthshire)
William Bedloe, 1650-1680: Adventurer and swindler, deeply implicated in the anti-Catholic 'Popish Plot'.
Edward Ernest Bowen, 1836-1901: Poet and campaigner for a University of Wales.
Sir Isambard Owen, 1859-1927: Physician and academic.
Ivor Walters, born 1907: Poet and local historian.

Richard Meade, born 1938: Olympic gold medallist, equestrian events 1968 and 1972: Welsh Sports Personality of the Year 1972.

CHIRK (Denbighshire)
Robert Jones, 1560-1615: Jesuit scholar.
Thomas Salusbury, 1612-1643: Poet.
Billy Meredith, 1874-1958: Outstanding Welsh football international and founder member of the Players' Union.
Neil Roderick Thomas, born 1968: Commonwealth Games gold medallist, gymnastics 1990.

CHURCH VILLAGE (Rhondda Cynon Taff)
Patricia Smith, born 1952: Folk musician.
Siwsann George, born 1956: Folk singer.

CHWILOG (Gwynedd)
John Thomas (Siôn Wyn o Eifion), 1787-1859: Bedridden poet.

CILFYNYDD (Rhondda Cynon Taff)
Merlyn Rees (Lord), born 1922: Senior Labour politician.
Sir Geraint Evans, 1922-1992: Acclaimed operatic baritone.
Gareth Owen, born 1922: Zoologist, educationist and public servant.
Glyn Davies, 1927-1976: Welsh rugby international.

Stuart Burrows, born 1933:
Popular opera and concert
tenor.

CILGERRAN
(Pembrokeshire)
Tom Mathias, 1865-1940: Folk
life photographer.

CIL-Y-CWM (Powys)
Morgan Rhys, 1716-1779:
Hymnwriter.

CLUNDERWEN
(Pembrokeshire)
Sir Roger Thomas, 1886-1960:
Authority on agriculture in
India.

CLYDACH (Swansea)
Morgan Watkins, 1878-1940:
Welsh language scholar.
Henry Lewis, 1889-1968:
Welsh language scholar
and academic.
Alun Oldfield-Davies, 1905-
1988: Controller BBC Wales
1945-1967:
W. Derek Bevan, born 1948:
Leading international
rugby referee, in charge of
World Cup Final, South
Africa 1995.
Elgan Rees, born 1954: Welsh
rugby international and
British Lion 1977 and 1980.
Floyd Havard, born 1965:
Champion super
featherweight boxer.

CLYDACH VALE (Rhondda
Cynon Taff)
Iorwerth Thomas, 1895-1966:
Labour MP for Rhondda
West.

Lewis Jones, 1987-1939:
Prominent Communist and
novelist.
Tommy Farr, 1914-1986:
Champion heavyweight
boxer.

CLYDEY (Pembrokeshire)
Erasmus Saunders, 1670?-
1724: Cleric and author.

CLYNNONG FAWR
(Gwynedd)
Morys Clynnog, c. 1525-1581:
Exiled Catholic theologian.

CNWCLAS (see
KNUCKLAS)

COCKETT (Swansea)
Will John, 1878-1955: Miners'
leader and Rhondda
Labour MP: in 1945 the last
MP from Wales to be
returned unopposed.

COGAN (Vale of Glamorgan)
Alan Harrington, born 1933:
Welsh football international.

COLWYN BAY (Conwy)
Geoffrey Nuttall, born 1911:
Religious historian.
Terry Jones, born 1942:
Comedy actor and writer.
Alun Michael, born 1943:
Senior Labour politician;
Secretary of State for Wales
1998. First Secretary of the
National Assembly for
Wales 1999-2000.
Timothy Dalton, born 1944:
Leading film actor.

CONWY (Conwy)

Richard Davies, 1501-1581: Bishop and Biblical scholar.

Robert Holland, c. 1556-1622?: Author.

John Williams, 1582-1650: Archbishop of York.

John Gibson, 1790-1866: Eminent painter.

Wyn Roberts (Lord), born 1930: Senior Conservative politician and television administrator.

CORRIS (Gwynedd)

David John Williams, 1896-1950: Children's writer, founder of 'Hwyl' comic.

John Disley, born 1928: Olympic bronze medalist, steeplechase 1952: Welsh Sports Personality of the Year 1955.

CORS CARON (Cardiganshire)

James Kitchener Davies, 1902-1952: Poet, author and Plaid Cymru politician.

CORWEN (Denbighshire)

Elena Puw Morgan, 1900-1973: Novelist.

Selyf Roberts, 1912-1995: Author, National Eisteddfod Prose Medal winner 1955.

Sir Charles Evans, 1918-1984: Surgeon, mountaineer and Principal of University College Bangor 1958-1984.

COWBRIDGE (Vale of Glamorgan)

Thomas Thomas, 1805-1881: College principal and leading British Baptist.

Thomas Rhondda Williams, 1860-1945: Powerful Calvinistic Methodist preacher.

Williams, Evan, 1912-2001: Grand National winning Jockey in 1937.

Sir Idwal Pugh, born 1918: Senior civil servant.

Anneka Rice, born 1958: Television personality.

COYCHURCH (Bridgend)

Arthur J. Williams, 1835-1911: Barrister and Liberal politician.

CRAIGCEFNPARC (Swansea)

William Williams (Crwys), 1875-1968: Poet, winner of National Eisteddfod Crown 1910, 1911 and 1919: Archdruid of Wales 1939-1947.

CREUDDYN (Cardiganshire)

Deio ap Ieuan Du, fl. 1460-1480: Poet, author of the line 'Y ddraig goch ddyry cychwyn' ('The red dragon will show the way'), now a patriotic motto.

CREUDDYN (Gwynedd)

William Williams (Creuddynfab), 1814-1869: Poet and author.

CRICCIETH (Gwynedd)

Sir Robert Armstrong-Jones, 1857-1943: Leading authority on mental health.

Gwilym Lloyd George (Lord Tenby), 1895-1967: Senior Conservative politician.

Lady Megan Lloyd George, 1902-1966: Liberal and Labour politician: in 1929 the first woman MP to be elected in Wales (Liberal, Anglesey).

Edward Davies Hughes, 1906-1963: Distinguished chemist.

William George (ap Llysor), born 1912: Poet, winner of the National Eisteddfod Chair 1974, Archdruid of Wales 1990-1993.

Guto Roberts, 1926-1999: Popular actor.

CRICKHOWELL (Powys)

Sir Charles Prestwood Lucas, 1853-1931: Leading colonial civil servant and historian.

Sir Walter Henry Cowan, 1871-1956: Admiral, took part in the Battle of Jutland 1916.

Reg Skrimshire, 1878-1963: Welsh rugby international, the only Welshman in the 1903 Lions South African tour.

Mark Wyatt, born 1957: Welsh rugby international.

CROES-YR-EIRIAS (Gwynedd)

William Davies, executed 1593: Catholic priest hanged, drawn and quartered at Beaumaris for treason.

CRUMLIN (Caerphilly)

David (Dai) Hayward, born 1934: Welsh rugby international.

Arthur Lewis, born 1941: Welsh rugby international, British Lion 1971.

CRYMMYCH (Carmarthenshire)

Milo Griffiths, 1843-1897: Noted sculptor.

CWM (Blaenau Gwent)

Edward Byles, born 1924: Opera and concert tenor.

Ryland Davies, born 1943: Opera and concert tenor.

Victor Spinetti, born 1943: Popular actor.

Mark Williams, born 1975: World snooker Champion 2000.

CWMAMAN (Rhondda Cynon Taff)

Alun Lewis, 1915-1944: Award-winning poet.

Elwyn Jones, 1923-1982: Television playwright.

Stuart Cable, born 1970: Member of 'Stereophonics' band.

Kelly Jones, born 1974: Member of 'Stereophonics' band.

Richard Jones, born 1974: Member of 'Stereophonics' band.

CWMAVON (Neath – Port Talbot)

William Abraham (Mabon), 1842-1922: Miners' leader and MP for Rhondda.

Mark Harcombe, 1876-1956:
Miners' leader and Labour
Party politician in Rhondda.
Emlyn Stephens, 1906-1963:
Director of Education for
Glamorgan 1944-1963.

CWMBRAN (Torfaen)
George Daggar, 1879-1950:
Miners' leader.
Chris Hallam, born 1934:
Champion disabled athlete.
David Thomas, 1954-1991:
Journalist and author,
killed in the Gulf War.

CWMBWRLA (Swansea)
Howell Thomas Evans, 1877-
1950: Historian.

CWMCARN (Caerphilly)
Sir Graham Sutton, 1903-
1977: Director-General,
Meteorological Office 1953-
1965.

CWMDU (Carmarthenshire)
Sir Daniel Lleufer Thomas,
1863-1940: Lawyer, magistrate
and Liberal politician.

CWMFELINFACH (Caerphilly)
Darren Thomas, born 1966:
Leading snooker player,
world amateur champion
1987.

CWM GOGERDDAN (Cardiganshire)
Dafydd Jones, 1711-1777:
Hymnwriter.

CWMGORS (Swansea)
Ann Griffiths, born 1935:
Harpist, in 1950 the
youngest person to be
admitted to membership of
the Gorsedd.

CWMGWRACH (Neath – Port Talbot)
David Richards, born 1954:
Welsh rugby international,
British Lion 1955 and 1959.
Kevin Hopkins, born 1961:
Welsh rugby international.

CWMPARC (Rhondda Cynon TafF)
John Evans, 1875-1961:
Miners' leader and Labour
MP for Ogmore.
Robert Thomas, 1926-1999:
Noted sculptor.
Ritchie Burnett, born 1958:
World darts champion 1995.
David Williams, born 1962:
Welsh football international.
Peter Williams, born 1962:
Welsh rugby international.

CWMTWRCH (Powys)
Thomas Eifion Hopkins
Williams, born 1923: Civil
engineer and public servant.
Clive Rowlands, born 1938:
Welsh rugby international:
Welsh Sports Personality of
the Year 1965.

CYMER (Rhondda Cynon Taf)
Gwyn Thomas, 1913-1981:
Novelist and playwright.

29

CYMER AFAN (Neath – Port Talbot)

Sir William Jenkins, 1871-1944: Miners' leader and Labour MP for Neath.

John Davies, born 1944: Award-winning poet.

CYNWYL ELFED (Carmarthenshire)

Howell Elvet Lewis (Elfed), 1860-1953: Poet and hymnwriter, winner of National Eisteddfod Chair 1894 and Crown 1880 and 1889: Archdruid of Wales 1924-1928.

D

DAFEN (Carmarthenshire)

Jeff Jones, born 1941: Glamorgan and England cricketer.

DEINIOLEN (Gwynedd)

Hugh Robert Jones, 1894-1930: Plaid Cymru pioneer.

Huw Lloyd Edwards, 1916-1975: Playwright.

Dafydd Orwig, 1928-1996: Welsh language activist.

Gwenlyn Parry, 1932-1991: Playwright.

DENBIGH (Denbighshire)

Humphrey Lloyd (Lhuyd), c. 1527-1568: Antiquary and cartographer.

Thomas Prys, c. 1564-1634: Poet, soldier and buccaneer.

Sir Richard Clough, 1550-1631: Creator of London's first efficient water supply.

Thomas Salusbury, 1564-1586: Executed for his part in the Babington Plot to assassinate Elizabeth I.

Hugh Holland, 1569-1633: Poet.

John Parry (Bardd Alaw), 1776-1881: Noted harpist, composer and collector.

Hugh Owen, 1784-1861: Soldier with distinguished service in the Portuguese army.

David Griffiths (Clwydfardd), 1800-1894: Poet, first official Archdruid of Wales 1876-1894.

Thomas Gee, 1815-1898: Publisher and social reformer.

Rhoda Broughton, 1840-1920: Novelist.

Sir Henry Morton Stanley (John Rowlands), 1841-1904: Journalist and African explorer.

A. G. Prys-Jones, 1888-1987: Poet, leading Anglo-Welsh writer.

Emlyn Hudson (Lord), born 1925: Lawyer, Liberal Democrat politician and public servant.

Tom Ellis Hooson, born 1932: Labour and Liberal Democrat politician.

Ieuan Wyn Jones, born 1949: AM, MP and President of Plaid Cymru from 2000.

Geraint Jarman, born 1950: Poet and singer.

DERI (Caerphilly)

Clifford Jones (Clifford Deri), 1901-1948: Noted operatic baritone.

Brian Price, born 1937: Welsh rugby international, British Lion 1966 and sports broadcaster.

John Uzzell, born 1942: Welsh rugby international.

DERLLYS COURT (Carmarthenshire)

John Vaughan, 1661-1722: Social and religious reformer.

DINAS (Rhondda Cynon Taff)

Ben Davies, 1840-1930: Poet.

DINAS POWYS (Vale of Glamorgan)

Sir Ivor B. Thomas, 1890-1955: Prominent Cardiff businessman and public servant: Welsh hockey international.

Julie Morgan, born 1944: Labour MP for Cardiff North: wife of Rhodri Morgan (qv).

Nicky Chinn, born 1972: Leading ice hockey player, England international.

DOLBENMAEN (Gwynedd)

Sir William Maurice, 1542-1622: MP who championed the union of England and Wales with Scotland under the name 'Great Britain'.

Sir John Owen, 1600-1666: Leading Royalist soldier in the Civil War.

DOLGARROG (Gwynedd)

Dave Powell, born 1944: Welsh football international.

DOLGELLAU (Gwynedd)

Robert Vaughan of Hengwrt, c. 1592-1667: Antiquary, collector of invaluable Welsh manuscripts.

Thomas Richards, 1806-1877: 'The father of Tasmanian journalism'.

Evan Jones (Ieuan Gwynedd), 1820-1852: Poet and prose writer.

John Jones, 1825-1887: Leading penillion performer.

Sir Cadwaladr Brynner Jones, 1872-1954: Leading agricultural scientist.

Llewellyn Wyn Griffiths, 1890-1977: Poet and novelist.

Tom Richards, 1908-1998: Journalist and playwright.

Ioan Bowen Rees, 1929-1999: Writer and public servant.

Heini Gruffudd, born 1946: Poet, novelist and author of Welsh leaners' books: brother of Robat Gruffudd (qv).

Nesta Wyn Jones, born 1946: Award-winning poet.

Alan Llwyd, born 1946: Poet and author: winner of National Eisteddfod Chair and Crown in both 1973 and 1976.

DOLWYDDELAN
(Gwynedd)
John Jones, 1796-1857:
Powerful Calvinistic
Methodist preacher.

DOWLAIS (Merthyr Tydfil)
Sir Josiah John Guest, 1785-
1852: Leading ironmaster.
Harry Evans, 1873-1914:
Noted choral conductor.
John Hughes, 1873-1932:
Hymnwriter whose
compositions include
'Cwm Rhondda'.
Evan Thomas Davies, 1879-
1969: Composer, conductor
and organist.
Sir Horace Evans, 1903-1963:
Royal physician.
Dyfnallt Morgan, 1917-1994:
Author and critic.
Sir Glanmor Williams, born
1920: Eminent historian.
Laura Ashley, 1925-1985:
Fashion designer.

Gwyn A. Williams, 1925-1995:
Popular historian and
broadcaster.
Glynne Jones, 1927-2000:
Leading choral conductor.

DUNVANT (Swansea)
Ceri Richards, 1903-1971:
Eminent painter.
Sir Granville Beynon, 1914-
1996: Distinguished physicist.
John Ormond, 1923-1990:
Award-winning poet and
leading documentary film
maker.

DYFFRYN ARDUDWY
(Gwynedd)
Edward Morgan Humphreys,
1882-1955: Journalist,
author and broadcaster.

DYFFRYN RHONDDA
(Neath – Port Talbot)
Steve Watkin, born 1964:
Glamorgan cricketer.

E

EBBW VALE (Blaenau Gwent)
Sir Edward (Ted) Williams,
1891-1963: Labour MP for
Ogmore 1931-1946: UK
High Commissioner in
Australia 1946-1952.
Eugene O'Callaghan, 1906-
1956: Welsh football
international.

Sir David Davies, born 1909:
Leading trade unionist:
first Chair of the Welsh
Development Agency 1976-
1979.
Jeff Banks, born 1943:
Fashion designer.
Robert Norster, born 1957:
Welsh rugby international,
British Lion 1983 and 1989.

Robert Ackerman, born 1961:
Welsh rugby international,
British Lion 1983.

EGLWYSILAN (Caerphilly)
William Edwards, 1719-1789:
Noted bridge builder,
especially of The Old
Bridge/Yr Hen Bont,
Pontypridd.

ERDDIG (Wrexham)
Philip Yorke, 1743-1804:
Antiquary, land improver
and lawyer.

ERWOOD (Powys)
Thomas William Chance,
1872-1954: Theologian,
Principal of South Wales
Baptist College, Cardiff.

F

FELINDRE
(Carmarthenshire)
Aneurin Talfan Davies, 1908-
1980: Poet, critic, senior
BBC administrator and
publisher.

FELINFOEL
(Carmarthenshire)
Dame Gwendoline Joyce
Trubshaw, 1887-1954: Social
worker and public servant.
Ifor Rees, 1893-1967: Awarded
the Victoria Cross in France
1917.
Phil Bennett, born 1948:
Welsh rugby international
and British Lion 1974 and
1977, sports commentator:
Welsh Sports Personality of
the Year 1977.

FERNDALE (Rhondda
Cynon Taff)
Roderick Jones, 1910-1992:
Opera and concert baritone.
Sir Stanley Baker, 1928-1976:
Leading actor and film
producer.
Alan Evans, 1950-1999: Leading
darts player: first holder of
World Masters title, 1965.
Paul Whitehouse, born 1958:
Successful comedy
actor/writer.

FFAIR RHOS (Cardiganshire)
Dafydd Jones, 1907-1991: Poet,
winner of the National
Eisteddfod Chair 1966.

FERRYSIDE
(Carmarthenshire)
Peter Roberts, born 1948:
Journalist, editor of the
'Cambrian News'.

FFESTINIOG (Gwynedd)

Morgan Llwyd, 1619-1692: Leading Dissenter.

Edward Stephen (Tanymarian), 1822-1885: Geologist and composer including 'Ystorm Tiberias', the first Welsh language oratorio.

Sir Lewis Casson, 1875-1969: Distinguished actor.

Sir Wyn Powel Wheldon, 1879-1961: Lawyer, soldier and public servant.

Daniel Howard Williams, 1894-1963: Aeronautics expert.

David Elwyn Jones, born 1945: Broadcaster and former Conservative agent.

FFYNNONGROEW (Flintshire)

Osian Ellis, born 1928: Distinguished harpist and academic.

Roy Vernon, born 1937: Welsh football international.

FISHGUARD (Pembrokeshire)

Jemima Nicholas, 1750-1832: Noted for her prominent role in surrender of French invasion force in 1797.

Sir Evan Davies Jones, 1859-1949: Coalition Liberal MP and public servant.

William Evans, 1864-1934: Head of the Rhondda-based Thomas and Evans grocery chain.

Arthur Wade-Evans, 1875-1964: Leading historian and archaeologist.

Fay Morgan, born 1946: Textile designer.

Jonathan Jones, born 1967: Champion powerboat racer.

FLEUR-DE-LLYS (Torfaen)

Victor Earle Nash-Williams, 1897-1955: Leading archaeologist.

FLINT (Flintshire)

Ron Hewitt, born 1928: Welsh international footballer.

FOUR CROSSES (Gwynedd)

Dilys Cadwaladr, 1902-1979: Poet, in 1953 the first woman to win a National Eisteddfod Crown.

FRON IW (Denbighshire)

William Alexander Madock, 1773-1828: Noted for his reclamation of the Traeth Mawr in Gwynedd and the building of the Cob there.

G

GAERWEN (Anglesey)
Dyfed Glyn Jones, born 1939:
 Novelist.

GARNANT (Swansea)
Claude Davey, 1908-2001:
 Welsh rugby international.
John Cale, born 1942: Star
 rock guitarist.
Hywel Bennett, born 1944:
 Leading actor.

GARTHMYL (Powys)
Arthur James Jenkins, 1809-
 1871: Author.
Arthur Humphreys-Owen,
 1836-1905: Liberal politician,
 educationist and advocate
 of a University of Wales.

GELLIGAER (Caerphilly)
Allan Rogers, born 1932:
 Labour MP for Rhondda.

GILFACH (Caerphilly)
Ivor Powell, born 1916: Welsh
 football international.

**GILFACH GOCH (Rhondda
 Cynon Taff)**
David Davies, 1871-1931:
 Mining engineer and noted
 geologist.
Sam Adams, born 1934: Poet,
 critic and editor.
Ian Hall, born 1946: Welsh
 rugby international.

GLAIS (Swansea)
Thomas John Morgan, 1907-
 1986: Welsh language scholar.

**GLANAMAN
 (Carmarthenshire)**
Ifor Thomas, 1877-1918:
 Geographer and educationist.
Dafydd Hywel, born 1946:
 Leading actor.
Nigel Davies, born 1965:
 Welsh rugby international.

**GLAN-YR-AFON
 (Gwynedd)**
D. Tecwyn Lloyd, 1914-1992:
 Lecturer, editor and award-
 winning author.

GLASBURY (Powys)
Colwyn Edward Vulliamy,
 1886-1971: Satirical writer.

**GLYNARTHEN
 (Cardiganshire)**
Gwawr Owen, born 1963:
 Director, Llangollen
 International Misical
 Eisteddfod, 1998.

**GLYNCEIRIOG
 (Denbighshire)**
Guto'r Glyn, c. 1435-1493: Major
 praise poet of the gentry.

**GLYNCORWG (Neath – Port
 Talbot)**
Glyn Williams, 1908-2001:
 President of South Wales
 Miners 1966-73.
Gerwyn Williams, born 1924:
 Welsh rugby international.

Rod Thomas, born 1947:
Welsh football international.

GLYNDYFRDWY
(Denbighshire)

Aled Vaughan, 1920-1989:
Television producer and
administrator.

GLYNNEATH (Neath – Port
Talbot)

Idris Glyn Prosser, 1907-1972:
Welsh rugby international
and founder of Welsh
Academicals rugby team.
Max Boyce, born 1943:
Popular singer-songwriter
and comedian.

GOGINAN (Cardiganshire)

Humphrey Owen Jones,
1878-1912: Noted chemist
and celebrated mountaineer.
William Ambrose Bebb, 1894-
1955: Writer and historian.

GOLDEN GROVE
(Carmarthenshire)

William Vaughan, 1578-1641:
Attempted unsuccessfully
to found a Welsh colony in
Newfoundland 1617-1637.

GORSEINON (Swansea)

David Alwyn Rees, 1911-
1974: Editor, sociologist
and educationist.
Sir Alun Talfan Davies, 1913-
2000: Lawyer, prominent
Liberal, publisher and public
servant.
Haydn Rees, born 1915: Lawyer
and public servant.

Roy Evans, born 1931:
General Secretary, Iron and
Steel Trades Confederation
1985.
Lewis Jones, born 1931: Welsh
rugby international.
Norman Gale, born 1939:
Welsh rugby international.
Gwynne Howell, born 1939:
Opera and concert bass.
Tristan Garel-Jones (Lord),
born 1941: Prominent
Conservative politician.
Michael Howard, born 1941:
Prominent Conservative
politician.
Nigel Jenkins, born 1949:
Award-winning author.
Robbie James, 1957-1998:
Welsh football international.
Richard Moriarty, born 1957:
Welsh rugby international.
Colin Jones, born 1959:
Champion welterweight
boxer, Welsh Sports
Personality of the Year, 1983.

GOWERTON (Swansea)

Ernest Jones, 1879-1958:
Psychoanalyst, biographer
and friend of Sigmund Freud.
Thomas Glyn Walters (Walter
Glynne), 1890-1970: Tenor –
one of the first British
singers to broadcast.
Ifor Davies, 1910-1982:
Labour MP for Gower.
Sir Ieuan Maddocks, born
1917: Physician and
educationist.
Haydn Tanner, born 1917:
Welsh rugby international.

Gwynne Walters, born 1928:
Leading international
rugby referee.

Onllwyn Brace, born 1932:
Welsh rugby international
and BBC Wales Head of
Sport.

Huw Tregelles Williams, born
1948: Organist and BBC
Wales Head of Music.

GOYTRE (Torfaen)

Harry Morgan, born 1930:
Welsh rugby international.

GREENFIELD (Flintshire)

Mike England, born 1941:
Welsh football international.

GRIFFITHSTOWN
(Torfaen)

D. G. James, born 1905:
Literary critic.

GROESLON (Gwynedd)

John Gwilym Jones, 1904-
1988: Author.

GWAELOD-Y-GARTH
(Cardiff)

Basil James, born 1918:
Leading lawyer.

GWAUN-CAE-GURWEN
(Carmarthenshire)

John Ellis Caerwyn Williams,
1912-1999: Celtic scholar.

Siân Phillips, born 1934:
Leading actress.

Gareth Edwards, born 1947:
Welsh rugby international,
British Lion 1968, 1971 and

1974: Welsh Sports
Personality of the Year 1974.

GWERNOGLE
(Carmarthenshire)

Thomas Evans (Tomos Glyn
Cothi), 1764-1833: Writer,
Unitarian and republican.

GWERNVALE (Powys)

Sir George Everest, 1790-1866:
Surveyor-general of India
after whom the world's
highest mountain is named.

GWYDIR (Gwynedd)

Sir John Wynn, 1553-1627:
Scholar and patron of poets.

GWYNFE (Carmarthenshire)

Sir John Williams, 1840-1926:
Founder of the National
Library of Wales.

GWYTHERIN (Denbighshire)

Robin Jones, born 1938:
Television presenter, S4C.

H

HALKYN (Flintshire)
Ann Clwyd, born 1937: Journalist and Labour MP and MEP.

HANMER (Flintshire)
Dafydd ap Edmwnd, fl. 1450-1490s: Major fifteenth century poet.

HARLECH (Gwynedd)
Ellis Wynne, 1671-1734: Poet who wrote the acclaimed 'Visions of the Sleeping Bard'.

HAROLDSTON (Pembrokeshire)
Sir John Perrot, 1530-1592: Elizabethan statesman, Lord Deputy of Ireland 1584-1588: reputed to have been an illegitimate son of Henry VIII.

HAVERFORDWEST (Pembrokeshire)
William Nichol, died 1588: Protestant martyr burnt at the stake in Haverfordwest for heresy.
Ernest Salter Davies, 1872-1955: Prominent educationist.
Gwen John, 1876-1939: Noted painter and sister of Augustus John (qv).

George Williams, 1879-1951: Leading Cardiff businessman and Conservative politician: supporter of capital city status for Cardiff.
Waldo Williams, 1904-1971: Poet and nationalist.
Robert Nisbet, born 1941: Short story writer.
David Llewellen, born 1960: Leading rally driver.
Gruff Rhys, born 1970: Member of 'Super Furry Animals' band.

HAWARDEN (Flintshire)
Anthony Millington, born 1943: Welsh football international.
Gary Speed, born 1969: Welsh football international.

HEBRON (Pembrokeshire)
Kevin Phillips, born 1961: Welsh rugby international and member of Welsh tug-of-war team.

HENDY (Carmarthenshire)
John Jenkins (Gwili), 1872-1936: Poet, winner of the National Eisteddfod Crown 1901: Archdruid of Wales 1932-1936.

HENGOED (Caerphilly)

Graham Moore, born 1941: Welsh football international: Welsh Sports Personality of the Year 1959.

HENLLAN (Pembrokeshire)

Richard Lewis, 1820-1905: Bishop of Llandaff who championed the appointment of Welsh-speaking clergy.

HENLLYS (Pembrokeshire)

George Owen, c. 1552-1613: Highly regarded writer and antiquary.

HENSOL CASTLE (Vale of Glamorgan)

David Jenkins, 1582-1663: Lawyer and prominent Royalist during the Civil War.

Sir Benjamin Hall, 1802-1867: Liberal politician after whom Parliament's 'Big Ben' is named.

HIRWAUN (Rhondda Cynon Taff)

David Wynne, 1900-1983: Noted composer.

HODGESTON (Pembrokeshire)

Thomas Young, 1507-1568: Archbishop of York 1561.

HOLYHEAD (Anglesey)

Francis Dodd, 1874-1917: Painter and etcher.

John Russell, 1893-1917: Awarded the Victoria Cross posthumously in France.

Thomas Wynford Rees (Dagger), 1898-1959: Major-general and public servant.

Ceinwen Rowlands, 1905-1983: Opera and concert singer.

Cledwyn Hughes (Lord), 1916-2001: Leading Labour politician: Secretary of State for Wales 1966-1968, Labour Leader in House of Lords 1982-1992.

Dawn French, born 1958: Popular comedy actress and writer.

HOLYWELL (Flintshire)

William Davies, 1814-1891: Palaeontologist, first recipient of the Murchison Medal of the Geological Society 1873.

Louise Myfanwy Thomas (Jane Ann Jones), 1906-1968: Novelist.

Jonathan Pryce, born 1947: Leading actor, winner of two Broadway Tony awards, 1979 and 1991.

J

JEFFREYSTON
(Pembrokeshire)
Rees (Rice) Powell, fl. 1638-
1665: Civil War
Parliamentary soldier.

K

KENFIG HILL (Bridgend)
Neale Doughty, born 1940:
Grand National winning
jockey 1984.
Howard Marks, born 1945:
Author of 'Mr Nice', his
best-selling autobiography
explaining his background
in drugs.

KIDWELLY
(Carmarthenshire)
Jack Anthony, 1890-1954:
Grand National winning
jockey 1911, 1915 and 1920.
Ednyfed Hudson Davies,
born 1929: Barrister:
Labour and SDP MP for
Conwy and Caerphilly:
Chair of Wales Tourist
Board 1976-1978.

Terry James, born 1934:
Conductor and composer
of film and television
music.
Ray Gravell, born 1951:
Welsh rugby international,
British Lion 1980;
broadcaster and actor;
National Eisteddfod Sword
Bearer from 1997.

KILVEY (Swansea)
Llewellyn Gwynne, 1863-
1957: Bishop of Egypt and
the Sudan for 26 years.

KNUCKLAS (Powys)
Vavasor Powell, 1617-1670:
Prominent Dissenter.
Malcolm Page, born 1947:
Welsh football international.

40

L

LAMPETER (Cardiganshire)
Simon Thomas, died 1743:
Author of only the second
book to be published in
Wales, 1718.
Idwal Jones, 1895-1937:
Playwright.
Eric Evans, 1901-1967:
Leading educationist.

LANDORE (Swansea)
R. M. (Dickie) Owen, 1876-1932:
Welsh rugby international.

**LAUGHARNE
(Carmarthenshire)**
Peter Williams, 1723-1796:
Methodist hymnwriter.
William Fuller, 1884-1974:
Awarded the Victoria Cross
in France 1914.

**LAVERNOCK (Vale of
Glamorgan)**
Sir Archibald Rowlands,
1892-1953: Distinguished
civil servant.

LEIGHTON (Powys)
Stephen Beattie, 1908-1942:
Awarded the Victoria Cross
posthumously at St
Nazaire, Brittany.

LIBANUS (Powys)
David Jones (Defynnog),
1865-1928: Author,
educationist and staunch
Welsh language supporter.

**LITTLE NEWCASTLE
(Pembrokeshire)**
Bartholemew Roberts (Black
Bart), c. 1682-1722: Pirate
killed by the Royal Navy
off West Africa.

**LLANAELHAIARN
(Gwynedd)**
Sir David Hughes Parry,
1893-1973: Leading legal
academic.

LLANAFAN FAWR (Powys)
T. Harri Jones, 1921-1965: Poet.

**LLANAMAN
(Carmarthenshire)**
Ryan Davies, 1937-1977:
Popular entertainer.

LLANARMON (Gwynedd)
Enenezer Thomas, 1802-1887:
Poet and critic.
John Ceiriog Hughes, 1832-
1887: Leading Welsh
language poet.

LLANARTH (Cardiganshire)
Daniel Silvan Evans, 1818-1913:
Lexicographer and poet.
Jenkin James, 1875-1948:
Educationist, Secretary to
the Council of the University
of Wales 1921-1948.

LLANARTH (Monmouthshire)

Ivor John Caradoc Owen
(Baron Treowen), 1851-
1933: Wealthy landowner,
soldier and Liberal MP.

LLANASA (Cardiganshire)

Ellis Gruffydd, fl. c. 1490-
1552: Soldier at Calais and
history chronicler.

LLANBADARN (Cardiganshire)

Sulien (the Wise), 1011-1091:
Noted scholar, Bishop of St
David's.

Rhigyfarch, c. 1056-1094:
Author of 'Life of St
David', son of Sulien.

John Mathias, 1837-1912:
Leading Cardiff shipowner.

LLANBADON (Monmouthshire)

Alfred Wallace, 1823-1913:
Naturalist whose theory of
evolution coincided with
Charles Darwin's.

LLANBEDR (Gwynedd)

Henry Lloyd, 1720-1783:
Soldier and author of a
noted book on military
engineering.

Rhiannon Davies, born 1921:
Award-winning novelist.

LLANBEDROG (Gwynedd)

Rowland Jones, 1722-1774:
Barrister and philologist
with mistaken ideas on the
Welsh language.

LLANBERIS (Gwynedd)

Griffith Hugh John, 1849-
1919: Noted musician.

Thomas Rowland Hughes,
1903-1949: Novelist and poet.

Gwilym Owen Williams,
1913-1990: Archbishop of
Wales 1971-1982.

LLANBLETHIAN (Vale of Glamorgan)

Sir Leoline Jenkins, 1625-
1685: Lawyer and 'second
founder' of Jesus College,
Oxford University.

LLANBRADACH (Caerphilly)

Morgan John Rees, 1760-1804:
Baptist and pioneer settler
in America.

Will Crews, 1893-1973: South
Wales miners' leader.

LLANBRYNMAIR (Powys)

Abraham Rees, 1743-1825:
Encyclopaedist: edited
'Chambers Encyclopaedia'
and 'The New Encyclopaedia'.

Ezekiel Hughes, 1866-1849:
Pioneer settler in America,
associate of President
Madison.

Samuel Roberts (S.R.), 1800-
1885: Publisher and reformer.

Iorwerth Peate, 1901-1982:
First curator of Welsh Folk
Museum, St Fagans.

Ithel Davies, 1904-1989:
Lawyer, writer and pacifist.

LLANCARFAN (Vale of Glamorgan)

David Davies (Dai'r Cantwr), 1812-1874: Rebecca rioter transported to Australia in 1843.

LLANDAFF (Cardiff)

Benjamin Hall, 1778-1817: founder of Rhymney Ironworks and first South Wales industrialist to become an MP: father of Sir Benjamin Hall (qv).

Sir William Goscombe John, 1860-1952: Distinguished sculptor.

Sir Ivor Algernon Atkins, 1869-1958: Organist and choirmaster.

Terry Nation, 1930-1997: Successful television writer and creator of the Daleks.

Robin John Hughes Simon, born 1947: Leading art critic.

LLANDDEINIOLEN (Gwynedd)

Erasmus Jones, 1817-1909: Novelist in the USA.

LLANDDERFEL (Gwynedd)

Edward Jones (Bardd o'r Brenin), 1752-1824: harpist and arranger of Welsh harp music.

Robert Jones Derfel, 1824-1905: Author of note.

LLANDDEUSANT (Carmarthenshire)

William Llywelyn Williams, 1867-1922: Journalist and historian.

Richard Vaughan (Ernest Lewis Thomas), 1904-1983: Successful novelist.

LLANDDEWI BREFI (Cardiganshire)

Sir David Davies, 1792-1865: Physician to King William IV.

LLANDDEWI ABER-ARTH (Cardiganshire)

Hywel Teifi Edwards, born 1934: Award-winning author, critic and literary historian.

LLANDDEWI SKIRRID (Monmouthshire)

Thomas James, c. 1593-c. 1835: Explorer of Hudson Bay in 1631: James Bay there is named after him.

LLANDDYFNAN (Anglesey)

Gruffydd ab Yr Ynad Goch, fl. 1280: Poet, author of a famous poem on the death of Llywelyn ap Gruffydd.

LLANDEGFAN (Anglesey)

Aled Jones, born 1970: Singer, celebrated boy soprano.

LLANDEILO (Carmarthenshire)

James Purdon Lewis Thomas (Viscount Cilcennan), 1903-1960: Conservative politician and administrator: Chair of TWW (commercial televison).

Elwyn Davies, 1908-1986: Educationist: President of the National Library of Wales.

Melville Richards, 1910-1973: Celtic scholar.

LLANDINAM (Powys)

David Davies, 1818-1890:
Railway and docks builder,
coalowner and philanthropist
known as 'Top Sawyer' and
'Davies the Ocean'.

David Davies (Lord), 1880-
1944: Landowner, Liberal
MP and philanthropist:
grandson of the above.

Gwendoline Davies, 1882-
1951: Sister of David and
philanthopist.

Margaret Davies, 1884-1963:
Sister of David and
philanthropist.

Mervyn Jones, 1911-1989:
Chair of nationalised Wales
Gas Board 1948-1970, and
Wales Tourist Board 1970-
1976: founder of the Civic
Trust in Wales.

LLANDOVERY
(Carmarthenshire)

Rhys Prichard (The Old Vicar),
1579-1644: Author of popular
'Canwyl y Cymry' ('The
Welshman's Candle') of
Christian precepts.

Rees Prydderch 1620?-1699:
Popular minister and
teacher: proverb collector.

William Williams (Pantycelyn),
1717-1791: Wales's most
outstanding hymnwriter.

Timothy Richard, 1845-1919:
Baptist missionary to China.

David Owen Evans, 1876-
1941: Lawyer, Liberal MP
and public servant.

LLANDRINDOD WELLS
(Powys)

Sydney Osborne Bufton,
1908-1993: Senior air force
officer, inventor of radionics:
Welsh hockey international.

Clement Jones, born 1915:
Writer and broadcaster.

David Gibson-Watt (Lord),
born 1918: Conservative
politician.

Richard Tudor, born 1959:
Leading yachtsman, round
the world races.

LLANDUDNO (Conwy)

Hugh Hughes, 1790-1863:
Artist and publisher.

William (Billy) Hughes) 1862-
1952: Australian Prime
Minister 1915-1923.

John Morgan, 1886-1957:
Archbishop of Wales 1949-
1957.

Aled Eames, 1921-1996:
Nautical historian.

Joey Jones, born 1953: Welsh
football international.

Neville Southall, born 1958:
Welsh international footballer:
Welsh Sports Personality of
the Year 1995.

LLANDULAS
(Denbighshire)

Lewis Valentine, 1893-1986:
Writer and Plaid Cymru
activist, jailed for his part in
the Pen-y-berth arson 1936.

LLANDYBIE
(Carmarthenshire)

Bowen Rees, 1857-1929:
Missionary to South Africa.

John Thomas Job, 1867-1938:
Poet.

Jenny Ogwen, born 1944:
Television presenter.

LLANDYFRYDOG
(Anglesey)

Hugh Hughes, 1693-1776:
Welsh language enthusiast.

LLANDYSSUL
(Cardiganshire)

Evan Pan Jones, 1834-1922:
Social reformer and
educationist.

John David Lewis, 1859-1914:
Publisher, founder of
Gwasg Gomer.

Sir John Lyn-Thomas, 1861-
1939: Distinguished
orthopaedic surgeon.

Sir James Smith, born 1913:
Leading Commonwealth
judge.

Hywel Davies, 1919-1965:
BBC Head of Programmes,
Cardiff.

Siân James, born 1932:
Award-winning novelist.

LLANDWROG (Gwynedd)

Griffith Davies, 1788-1855:
Leading actuary and
mathematician.

LLANEDI (Carmarthenshire)

John Walters, 1721-1797:
Lexicographer.

LLANEGRYN (Powys)

Maredudd Evans, born 1919:
Musician and senior BBC
Wales administrator.

LLANELIDAN
(Denbighshire)

Edward Jones, executed 1590:
Catholic hanged in London
for harbouring a priest.

Walter Wingfield, 1833-1912:
Originated the game which
became modern lawn tennis.

LLANELLI (Carmarthenshire)

John Graham Chambers,
1843-1883: Sportsman,
devised the Queensberry
Rules for boxing.

David Davies, 1862-1932:
Journalist and author.

Charles Alfred Howell Green,
1864-1944: Archbishop of
Wales 1934-1944.

James Dickson Innes, 1887-
1914: Noted painter.

James Griffiths, 1890-1975:
Miners' leader and Labour
politician: first Secretary of
State for Wales 1964-1966.

Dai Davies, 1897-1976:
Glamorgan cricketer.

Sir Tom O'Brien, 1900-1970:
Labour MP, trade union
officer and public servant.

Theodore Nicholl, 1902-1973:
Poet and novelist.

Emrys Cleaver, 1904-1985:
Popular actor.

Emrys Davies, 1904-1975:
Glamorgan cricketer.

Elwyn Jones (Lord), 1909-1989:
Leading lawyer, Labour Lord
Chancellor 1974-1979.

Llywelyn Williams, 1911-1965:
Labour MP for Abertillery.

Haydn Davies, born 1912:
Glamorgan cricketer and
leading squash player.

Clifford Evans, 1912-1985: Leading actor.

Geraint Bowen, born 1915: Poet, winner of National Eisteddfod Chair 1946; Archdruid of Wales 1978-1981.

Bill Clement, born 1915: Welsh rugby international, British Lion 1938 and long-serving Secretary of the Welsh Rugby Union 1956-1981.

Handel Rogers, born 1917: President of the Welsh Rugby Union 1975-1976.

Donald Swann, born 1923: Popular song writer and performer.

Ioan Evans, 1927-1984: Labour and Co-operative MP for Cynon Valley.

Rachel Roberts, 1927-1980: Actress: Hollywood Oscar nomination for Best Supporting Actress 1963.

Ivor Richard (Lord), born 1932: Labour politician, European Community Commissioner 1981-1984: Labour Party leader in House of Lords 1992-1998.

Sir John Meurig Thomas, born 1932: Distinguished chemist and educationist: Director of the Royal Institute of Great Britain.

Shirley Jones, born 1936: Leading table tennis player.

David Quentin Bowen, born 1938: Leading earth scientist.

Derek Quinnell, born 1949: Welsh rugby international, British Lion 1971 and 1977.

Terry Griffiths, born 1949: Leading snooker player; world champion 1979: Welsh Sports Peronality of the Year 1979.

Keith Allen, born 1952: Leading actor.

Phil May, born 1956: Welsh rugby international.

Rhodri Thomas, born 1962: Folk musician, member of 'Bwchadanas' group.

Neil Haddock, born 1964: Champion super-featherweight boxer.

Scott Quinnell, born 1972: Welsh rugby international, British Lion 1997 and 2001, son of Derek.

LLANERCH-Y-MEDD (Anglesey)

Richard Parry (Gwalchmai), 1803-1897: Independent minister, author, poet and editor.

LLANERFYL (Powys)

Gwyn Erfyl Jones, born 1924: Poet and editor.

Siân James, born 1961: Folk singer.

LLANFACHREDD (Powys)

William Williams (o'r Wern) 1781-1840: Leading Independent minister.

Evan Gwyndaf Evans, 1913-1986: Poet, winner of National Eisteddfod Chair 1935, Archdruid of Wales 1966-1969.

LLANFAIR CAREINION (Powys)

Emrys Evans, born 1924:
Banker and public servant.
Dillwyn Owen, 1922-1999:
Popular actor.

LLANFAIR FECHAN (Gwynedd)

Dilwyn Owen, 1922-99:
Poular actor.

LLANFAIRMATHAFARN EITHAF (Anglesey)

Goronwy Owen (Goronwy
Ddu o Fôn), 1723-1769:
Leading eighteenth century
poet.

LLANFAIR TALHAEARN (Denbighshire)

John Jones, 1810-1869: Poet
and architect.

LLANFECHAIN (Powys)

Walter Davies (Gwallter
Mechain), 1761-1849: Poet
and antiquary.
David Thomas, 1880-1967:
Historian, Labour Party
and Workers' Educational
Association pioneer.

LLANFECHELL (Anglesey)

William Buckley, 1691-1760:
Diarist of contemporary life
in Anglesey.

LLANFERRES (Denbighshire)

John Davies, c. 1567-1644:
Renaissance scholar.

LLANFIHANGEL ABERCYWYN (Carmarthenshire)

David Charles, 1762-1834:
Noted Methodist hymnwriter.

LLANFIHANGEL BRYN PABUAN (Powys)

Thomas Price (Carnhuanawc),
1787-1848: Historian and
eisteddfodwr.

LLANFIHANGEL GENAU'R GLYN (Cardiganshire)

Lewis Thomas, 1832-1913:
'The coal king of Queensland'.

LLANFIHANGEL GLYN MYFYR (Denbighshire)

Madog ap Gwallter, fl. 13th
century: Poet and Franciscan.
Owen Jones (Owen Myfyr),
1741-1814: Antiquary:
founder of the Gwyneddigion
Society in London, 1772.

LLANFIHANGEL IORARTH (Carmarthenshire)

Sarah Jacobs, 1857-1869: 'The
Welsh fasting girl' said to
have lived for over two years
without food or drink. Her
parents were imprisoned
after her death.

LLANFIHANGEL TRE'R BEIRDD (Anglesey)

William Jones, 1675?-1749:
Distinguished mathematician:
first person to use π to denote
ratio of the circumference

of a circle to its radius: Vice-president of the Royal Society.

Lewis Morris, 1701-1765/ Richard Morris, 1703-1779/ William Morris, 1705-1763/ John Morris, 1706-1740: Of these talented Morris brothers, Lewis was the most able. A scholar and surveyor, he was also a founder of London's Cymmrodorion Society.

LLANFIHANGEL-YNG-NGWYNFA (Powys)

Ann Griffiths, 1776-1805: Celebrated Methodist hymnwriter.

LLANFIHANGEL-Y-PENNANT (Gwynedd)

William Owen Pughe, 1759-1835: Lexicographer with erroneous ideas on derivation of Welsh words.

Mary Jones, 1784-1872: Admired for her 25 mile walk barefooted to Bala to buy a Bible from Thomas Charles (qv).

Meirion William Evans, 1826-1883: Pioneer of Welsh language publications in Australia and New Zealand.

LLANFIHANGEL-YR-ARTH (Cardiganshire)

Caradoc Evans, 1878-1945: Controversial playwright and novelist.

LLANFROTHEN (Gwynedd)

Bob Owen (Croesor), 1885-1962: Antiquarian book collector of renown.

Robin Llywelyn, born 1958: Author, winner of the National Eisteddfod Prose Medal 1992: winner of Arts Council of Wales Welsh Book of the Year Award 1993.

LLANFRYNACH (Powys)

Thomas Evan Nicholas (Niclas y Glais), 1878-1971: Poet and pacificist.

LLANFWROG (Denbighshire)

Isaac Foulkes, 1836-1904: Publisher, journalist and author.

LLANFYLLIN (Powys)

Charles Lloyd, 1637-1698: Leading Quaker.

Thomas Lloyd, 1640-1690: Leading Quaker who became deputy to the governor of Pennsylvania.

Sir Percy Watkins, 1871-1946: Senior civil servant.

E. Alfred Jones, 1872-1943: Authority on religious silver plate and furniture.

Clement Davies, 1884-1962: Liberal MP for Montgomery, leader of the Liberal Party 1945-1956.

Elizabeth Vaughan, born 1937: Leading operatic soprano and teacher.

LLANFYNYDD
(Carmarthenshire)
John Dyer, 1699?-1757:
Acclaimed poet.
David Ellis Evans, born 1930:
Celtic scholar.

LLANGADFAN
(Carmarthenshire)
William Jones, 1726-1795:
'The Welsh Voltaire':
advocate of a national
eisteddfod.
John Cadvan Davies (Cadfan),
1846-1923: Poet, winner of
National Eisteddfod Crown
1884, 1886 and 1887:
Archdruid of Wales 1923-
1924.
William Emrys Evans, born
1924: Banker and public
servant.

LLANGADOG
(Carmarthenshire)
Arthur Rees, 1912-1998:
Welsh rugby international:
Chief Constable of both
Denbighshire and
Staffordshire.
Wyndham Roy Davies, 1926-
1984: Pharmaceutical
authority and Conservative
MP.

LLANGADWALADR
(Anglesey)
Owen Lewis, 1533-1595:
Bishop of Cassano, Naples:
prominent Catholic exile.

LLANGAMMARCH WELLS
(Powys)
John Penry 1563?-1593:
Puritan leader, 'The
Morning Star of the Welsh
Reformation', beheaded in
Surrey for heresy.

LLAN-GAN (Vale of
Glamorgan)
John Pritchard, 1817-1886:
Noted architect, restorer of
Llandaff Cathedral in mid
nineteenth century.
David Dilwyn John, 1901-1995:
Director of the National
Museum of Wales 1948-1968.

LLANGATTOCK
(Monmouthshire)
Sir Thomas Morgan, 1604-
1679: Distinguished soldier
in continental wars.

LLANGATTOCK VIBON
AVEL (Monmouthshire)
Charles Rolls, 1877-1910: Co-
founder of the famous car
company; first Briton to be
killed in a flying accident.

LLANGEFNI (Anglesey)
Richard Davies, 1818-1896:
One of the first Nonconformist
MPs in Wales.
Sir Kyffin Williams, born
1918: Distinguished artist.
William Elwyn Williams, born
1931: Leading mathematician.
Hywel Gwynfryn, born 1942:
Television and radio
broadcaster.

49

LLANGEINOR (Bridgend)

Richard Price, 1723-1791:
Radical political theorist
admired by American and
French revolutionaries.

LLANGEINWEN (Anglesey)

Sir Hugh Owen, 1804-1881:
Distinguished educationist,
campaigner for a University
College at Aberystwyth.

LLANGEITHO (Cardiganshire)

Evan David Jones, 1903-1987:
Librarian, National Library
of Wales.

LLANGELYNIN (Gwynedd)

Rhys (Arise) Evans, c. 1607-
1660: Religious extremist.
John Morgan, 1688-1733:
Scholar and poet.
Sir Vincent Evans, 1851-1934:
Prominent London journalist,
supported revival of London
Cymmrodorion Society and
the National Eisteddfod.

LLANGENNECH (Carmarthenshire)

Rhys Davies, 1877-1954:
Trade union leader and
Labour MP.
Rhys Gabe, 1880-1967: Welsh
rugby international and
British Lion 1904.
Hubert Rees, born 1923:
Leading botanist.

LLANGERNYW (Conwy)

Howell Roberts, 1840-1922:
Poet, preacher and inventor.
Sir Henry Jones, 1852-1922:
Philosopher and educationist.

LLANGIAN (Gwynedd)

William Owen, 1530?-1587:
Poet of note.

LLANGIWG (Swansea)

John Dyfnallt Owen, 1883-
1956: Poet, winner of
National Eisteddfod Chair
1907: Archdruid of Wales
1954-1956.

LLANGLYDWEN (Carmarthenshire)

David Evans, born 1937:
general Secretary of the
Samaritans 1984.

LLANGOEDMOR (Powys)

John Jenkins (Ifor Ceri), 1770-
1829: Poet, musicologist,
eisteddfod pioneer.

LLANGOLLEN (Denbighshire)

Gruffudd Hiraethog, died
1564: Major poet and
Deputy Herald of Wales for
College of Arms.
Huw Morys, 1622-1709: Poet.
Jonathan Hughes, 1721-1805:
Poet.
W. S. Gwynne Williams, 1896-
1978: Founding organiser
of the Llangollen
International Eisteddfod.
Emlyn Hugh Garner Evans,
1911-1963: Liberal MP and
editor.
Robyn Lewis, born 1929:
Author, winner of National
Eisteddfod Prose Medal 1979.

LLANGORWEN (Cardiganshire)

Isaac Williams, 1802-1865: Poet and controversial theologian.

LLANGRANNOG (Cardiganshire)

Sarah Jane Rees, 1839-1916: Navigation teacher and temperance movement leader.

Alun Jeremiah Jones (Alun Cilie), 1897-1975: Poet.

John Geraint Jenkins, born 1929: Curator, Museum of Welsh Life, St Fagans, 1987.

LLANGRISTIOLUS (Anglesey)

Thomas Jerman Jones, 1833-1890: Calvinistic Methodist Missionary to Assam.

Ifan Gruffydd, 1896-1971: Author.

William Robert Lewis, born 1918: Playwright.

LLANGUA (Monmouthshire)

George Ethelbert Sayce, 1875-1953: Journalist and mid Wales newspaper owner.

LLANGURIG (Powys)

David Arthur Lewis, 1880-1942: Historian.

LLANGWM (Monmouthshire)

Walter Cradock, c. 1610-1659: Prominent Dissenter, established the first chapel in Cardiff.

LLANGWNADL (Gwynedd)

John G. Williams, born 1915: Prose writer and award-winning novelist.

LLANGYBI (Gwynedd)

John Robert Williams, born 1914: Journalist and broadcaster.

LLANGYFELACH (Swansea)

Evan John Walters, 1893-1951: Noted artist.

LLANGYNHAFAL (Denbighshire)

Robert Jones, 1769-1833: Writer and friend of Wordsworth.

LLANGYNOG (Carmarthenshire)

Huw Humphreys Davies, born 1940: Television producer.

LLANGYNWYD (Bridgend)

Will Hopkyn, 1700-1741: Poet remembered for the song 'Bugeilio'r Gwenith Gwyn'.

Ann Maddocks (née Thomas), 1704-1727: Reputed tragic figure through her supposed love for Will Hopcyn.

LLANGYNYW (Powys)

Thomas Jones, 1810-1849: Calvinistic Methodist missionary to Assam.

LLANHILLETH (Blaenau Gwent)

Ray Gunter, 1909-1977: Senior Labour politician and trade unionist.

LLANIDAN (Gwynedd)

Henry Rowlands, 1655-1723: Antiquary.

LLANIDLOES (Powys)

Richard Gwyn, c. 1557-1585:
A Catholic hanged, drawn
and quartered at Wrexham
for heresy.

Richard Mills, 1809-1844:
Composer and collecter of
Welsh hymns and anthems.

Abraham Matthews, 1832-1899:
Pioneer settler in Patagonia:
author of a book on the
history of the Welsh colony.

Gwilym Richard Tilsley (Tilsli),
1911-1997: Winner of National
Eisteddfod Chair in 1950
and 1957: Archdruid of
Wales 1969-1972.

Elinor Bennett, born 1943:
Noted harpist: wife of
Dafydd Wigley (qv).

LLANILAR (Denbighshire)

Robert Evan Roberts, born
1912: Senior YMCA
administrator and public
servant.

LLANLLECHID (Gwynedd)

Gwilym Rees Hughes, born
1930: Poet and editor.

LLANLLUGAN (Powys)

William Baxter, 1650-1723:
Lexicographer with
mistaken ideas on the
origin of Welsh words.

LLANLLWCHHAEAERN (Powys)

Geraint Goodwin, 1903-1941:
Noted author.

LLANLLYFNI (Gwynedd)

Robert Roberts (Silyn), 1871-
1930: Poet, socialist and
adult education pioneer.

LLANNEFYDD (Denbighshire)

Thomas Edwards (Twm o'r
Nant), 1738-1810: Writer of
interludes –a popular form
of entertainment.

Thomas Robert Jones, 1802-
1856: Founder of the True
Invorites Friendly Society
in 1836, the first friendly
society in Wales.

LLANON (Denbighshire)

Timothy Rees, 1974-1939:
Bishop of Llandaff 1031-1939.

LLANOVER HALL (Monmouthshire)

Augusta Hall (Lady
Llanover), 1804-1896: Welsh
culture enthusiast:
originator of 'traditional'
Welsh female costume.

LLANRHAEDR-YM-MOCHNANT (Powys)

Griffith Hartwell Jones, 1859-
1944: Historian.

LLANRHYCHWYN (Gwynedd)

Robert Williams (Trebor Mai),
1830-1877: Poet.

LLANRHYSTED (Carmarthenshire)

J. M. Edwards, 1903-1978:
Poet, winner of the
National Eisteddfod Corwn
1937, 1941 and 1944.

LLANRUG (Gwynedd)

Hugh Rowlands, 1828-1909: Awarded the Victoria Cross during the Crimean War, 1854: the first Welshman to win the V.C.

John David Rheinallt Jones, 1884-1953: Authority on race relations in South Africa.

LLANRWST (Gwynedd)

Edmund Prys, 1544-1623: Biblical scholar and translator.

Inigo Jones, 1573-1652: Eminent architect. (His birth here is not certain).

Robert Griffith Berry, 1869-1945: Writer.

Peter Thomas (Lord), born 1920: Conservative politician: Secretary of State for Wales 1970-1974.

T. Glynne Davies, 1926-1988: Broadcaster, award-winning poet and novelist.

Wyn Jones, born 1926: Colonial administrator and public servant.

Dafydd Elis-Thomas (Lord), born 1946: Plaid Cymru leader: First President Welsh Assembly 1999.

Geraint Glynne Davies, born 1953: Member of 'Ar Log' folk group.

LLANRHYSTYD (Cardiganshire)

Evan Evans, died 1928: Co-designer of the Australian national flag.

LLANSADWRN (Anglesey)

Peter Williams, 1723-1796: Early Methodist Revival leader.

Thomas Williams, 1737-1796: Industrialist known as 'the Copper King' and 'Twm Chwarae Teg' ('Tom Fair Play').

James Williams, 1790-1872: Cleric and founder of the Anglesey Association for the Preservation of Life from Shipwrecks.

LLANSAINT (Carmarthenshire)

Gerald Davies, born 1945: Welsh rugby international, British Lion in 1973 and 1977 and sports journalist.

LLANSAMLET (Swansea)

Idris Evans, 1890-1952: Head of BBC Music Department in Cardiff.

Tom Parker, 1891-1967: Welsh rugby international.

Jack Kelsey, 1929-1992: Welsh football international.

LLANSANNAN (Denbighshire)

Tudur Aled, c. 1460-c. 1526: Last great pencerdd or master poet.

William Salesbury, c. 1520-c. 1599: Cleric, translator of the New Testament into Welsh.

William Rees (Gwilym Hiraethog), 1802-1888: 'The father of the Welsh press'.

Sir William Lloyd Mars Jones, 1915-1999: Judge: prosecuting barrister in the notorious Moors Murders case 1966.

LLANSANTFFRAED (Denbighshire)

Jon Jones, 1790-1855: Printer and first publisher of 'Yr Amserau' Welsh newspaper.

LLANSANTFFRAED (Powys)

Thomas Vaughan, 1621-1666: Alchemist and poet.

Henry Vaughan (The Silurist), 1622-1695: Noted author.

Cledwyn Hughes, 1920-1978: Novelist and topographical writer.

Charles Cuthbert Powell Williams (Baron Williams of Elvet), born 1933: Labour politician, authority on banking and industry.

LLANSANTFFRAID-YM-MECHAIN (Powys)

Gwerful Mechain, fl. 1462-1500: Important late medieval woman poet.

LLANSAWEL (Carmarthenshire)

Mary Owen, 1796-1875: Hymnwriter.

LLANTARNAM (Monmouthshire)

Alun Gwynne Jones (Lord Chalfont), born 1919: Writer on defence matters, Labour politician and Chair of the Radio Authority.

LLANTRISANT (Anglesey)

Gruffudd Gryg, fl. 1357-1370: Talented poet: a noted poem on a pilgrimage to Santiago de Compostella, Galicia, is usually attributed to him.

LLANTRISANT (Rhondda Cynon Taff)

Sir David Treharne, 1849-1907: Prominent businessman in London: Lord Mayor there 1891.

William Llywellyn, 1850-1925: Businessman and leading Liberal local politician.

LLANTRITHYD (Vale of Glamorgan)

Thomas John, 1834-1893: Foreman of Bute workshops during reconstruction of Cardiff Castle and Castell Coch: father of Sir William Goscombe John (qv).

LLANTWIT MAJOR (Vale of Glamorgan)

Llywelyn ap Rhisart (Lewys Morganwg), fl. 1520-1565: Leading Glamorgan poet.

John Morgan, 1889-1970: Leading South Wales industrialist and founder member of Welsh National Opera.

LLANTYDEWI (Pembrokeshire)

Joseph Harris (Gomer), 1773-1825: Writer and printer: founded the first Welsh language newspaper 'Seren Gomer' 1814.

LLANUWCHLLYN (Gwynedd)

John Davies, died 1694: One of the last of the Welsh family bards.

Robert Thomas (ap Fychan), 1809-1880: Poet and man of letters.

Michael D. Jones, 1822-1898: Promoter of the Welsh settlement in Chubut, Patagonia – Y Wladfa.

Sir Owen Morys Edwards, 1858-1920: Educationist, author and editor: first Chief Inspector of Schools in Wales.

Sir Ifan ab Owen Edwards, 1895-1970: Founder of Urdd Gobaith Cymru 1922: son of Sir Owen.

LLANWINIO (Carmarthenshire)

Jacob Thomas, 1833-1896: Awarded the Victora Cross during the Crimean War 1857.

William Evans (Wil Ifan), 1883-1968: Poet, winner of the National Eisteddfod Crown in 1913, 1917 and 1925: Archdruid of Wales 1947-1950.

LLANWENOG (Cardiganshire)

Abel Morgan, 1673-1722: Baptist minister: author of the second book in Welsh published in America.

LLANWONNO (Rhondda Cynon Taff)

Griffith Morgan (Guto Nyth Brân), 1700-1737: Champion runner.

Richard Griffiths, 1756-1826: First person to begin systematic exploitation of Rhondda coal 1790.

Naunton Wayne, 1901-1978: Popular actor.

LLANWRTYD (Powys)

David Williams, 1779-1874: Considered the oldest minister still active in Wales on his death aged 95.

Thomas Powell, 1845-1922: First Professor of Celtic at University College, Cardiff.

LLANYBYDDER (Carmarthenshire)

Lewis Glyn Cothi, fl. 1447-1486: One of the greatest fifteenth century poets.

John Gwenogvryn Evans, 1852-1930: Palaeographer, Welsh language scholar.

LLANYCEFN (Pembrokeshire)

David Williams, 1900-1978: Leading historian.

LLAN-YM-MAWDDWY (Gwynedd)

David Roberts (Telynor Mawddwy), 1871-1956: Harpist, singer and author.

Alfred George Edwards, 1848-1937: First Archbishop of Wales 1920-1934.

LLANYMYNECH (Powys)

Richard Roberts, 1789-1864: Inventor in a wide range of activities.

LLANYSTUMDWY (Gwynedd)

Robert Williams (Robert ap Gwilym Ddu), 1766-1830: Poet and hymnwriter.

David Owen, 1784-1841: Poet.

William George, 1865-1967: Solicitor, author and public servant.

William Samuel Jones, born 1920: Playwright and short story writer.

Robert Tudor Jones, 1921-1998: Leading Nonconformist theologian and nationalist: award-winning author.

LLAY (Wrexham)

Terry Hennessey, born 1942: Welsh football international.

LLEDROD (Cardiganshire)

Evan Evans (Ieuan Brydydd Hir), 1731-1788: Welsh language scholar and poet: published the first major collection of early Welsh poetry in 1764.

LLITHFAEN (Gwynedd)

Griffith P. Williams, 1888-1994: Published his autobiography when aged 100.

LLWYNDERW (Carmarthenshire)

William Lewis, 1652-1722: Genealogist and antiquary.

LLWYNYHENDY (Carmarthenshire)

Douglas Bassett, born 1927: Director, National Museum of Wales 1977-1985.

Terry Davies, born 1933: Welsh rugby international, British Lion 1950.

LLWYNYPIA (Rhondda Cynon Taff)

Annie Powell, 1906-1986: Britain's first and only Communist Party mayor – of Rhondda 1979-1980.

John Davies, born 1938: Historian, author and broadcaster.

Robat Gruffudd, born 1943: Publisher and novelist: brother of Heini Gruffudd (qv).

John Davies, born 1952: Commonwealth Games silver medallist, steeplechase 1974.

LOUGHOR (Carmarthenshire)

Evan Roberts, 1878-1951: Leader of the last major religious revival in Wales 1904-1905.

Ivor Jones, 1901-1982: Welsh rugby international, British Lion 1930, President Welsh Rugby Union 1968-1969.

Irma Chilton, born 1930: Prize-winning novelist.

Leighton James, born 1953: Welsh football international.

M

MACHEN (Caerphilly)

Malcolm Thomas, born 1929:
Welsh rugby international,
British Lion 1954 and 1957.

Ron Davies, born 1946: Senior
Labour politician: Secretary
of State for Wales 1997-
1998: lead 'Yes' devolution
campaign 1997 and guided
Welsh Assembly Bill
through Parliament 1998.

MACHYNLLETH (Powys)

Hugh Williams, 1796-1874:
Lawyer and leading Chartist.

Owen Owen, 1847-1910:
Department store owner.

Emyr Jenkins, born 1938:
National Eisteddfod Director,
BBC producer, father of Ffion
Jenkins – wife of William
Hague, Conservative Party
leader from 1997.

MADRYN (Gwynedd)

Sir Love Jones-Parry, 1781-
1853: Surveyed Chubut
Patagonia, for Welsh settlers:
squire of Madryn, Llŷn,
after which Puerto Madryn,
Argentina, is named.

John Owen William (Pedrog),
1853-1932: Poet, winner of
National Eisteddfod Chair
1891, 1895 and 1900;
Archdruid of Wales 1928-
1932.

MAELOR (Flintshire)

Matthew Gough (Goch),
1386-1450: Distinguished
soldier.

Bernard Warburton-Lee,
1895-1940: Awarded the
Victoria Cross posthumously,
Royal Navy action at Narvik,
Norway.

MAENCLOCHOG (Pembrokeshire)

James Jubilee Young, 1887-1963:
Powerful Baptist preacher.

MAENTWROG (Gwynedd)

Morgan Llwyd, 1619-1659:
Puritan author.

John Elfed Jones, born 1933:
Leading businessman and
public servant.

MAESTEG (Bridgend)

Evan Williams, 1887-1947:
Miners' leader.

Sir Rhys Hopkin Morris,
1888-1956: Barrister,
Director of BBC Welsh
Region 1936-1945.

Sir Beddoe Rees, died 1931:
Coalowner and Cardiff
shipowner: Liberal MP.

Sir David Davies, 1896-1991:
Chair of Wales Tourist
Board 1965-1970.

Idris Cox, 1900-1989: Leading
Communist.

Brinley Richards (Brinli), 1904-1981: Poet, winner of the National Eisteddfod Chair 1951: Archdruid of Wales 1972-1975.

Vernon Watkins, 1906-1967: Leading poet.

Gwyneth Petty, born 1931: Actress.

Alun Protheroe, born 1934: Senior television administrator.

Ray Hopkins, born 1946: Welsh rugby international.

John Hopkins, born 1953: Glamorgan cricketer.

Gwyn Evans, born 1957: Welsh rugby international.

Mark Davies, born 1958: Welsh rugby international.

Siân Lloyd, born 1958: Television personality.

MAES-Y-GARNEDD (Gwynedd)

John Jones, 1597-1660: Parliamentary soldier and brother-in-law of Oliver Cromwell: executed as regicide at the Restoration.

MALLWYD (Powys)

John Rice Jones, 1759-1824: Prominent pioneer settler in the American mid-west, businessman and lawyer.

MANCOT (Flintshire)

Sioned Edwards Williams, born 1953: Noted harpist.

Myrddin ap Dafydd, born 1956: Publisher and poet, winner of the National

Eisteddfod Chair 1990 and Urdd National Eisteddfod Chair 1974.

Kevin Radcliffe, born 1960: Welsh international footballer.

MANORBIER (Pembrokeshire)

Gerald of Wales (Geraldus Cambrensis), c. 1146-1223: Cleric and major writer whose work is an invaluable source of information on twelfth century Wales and Ireland.

MARGAM (Neath – Port Talbot)

Edward Dafydd, c. 1600-1678: Celebrated Glamorgan poet.

John Morgan Jones, 1861-1935: Leading Calvinistic Methodist, author and pacifist.

MARIAN GLAS (Anglesey)

Hugh Griffith, 1912-1980: Popular actor, winner of Hollywood Oscar for Best Supporting Actor 1967.

MARKHAM (Torfaen)

David Nash, born 1939: Welsh rugby international, British Lion 1962.

MELLTEYRN (Gwynedd)

Henry Rowland, 1551-1626: Bishop of Bangor, founder of Botwnnog Grammar School.

MENAI BRIDGE (Anglesey)

John Evans (Y Bardd Cocos),
1827-1888: Doggerel writer.

Jane Helen Rowlands, 1871-1955:
Teacher and missionary to
India.

Alun Owen, 1925-1994:
Leading television playwright.

MERTHYR TYDFIL

Penry Williams, 1802-1885:
Noted artist.

John Hughes, 1814-1889:
Ironmaster in the Ukraine.

Sir Samuel Griffiths, 1824-1920:
Premier of Queensland 1883.

David Watkin Jones, 1832-
1905: Poet and historian.

Sir William Thomas Lewis
(Lord Merthyr), 1837-1914:
Coalowner.

Joseph Parry, 1841-1903:
Renowned composer and
academic.

Charles Radcliffe, 1862-1926:
Cardiff shipowner.

Henry Seymour Berry (Lord
Buckland), 1877-1928:
Coalowner and philanthropist.

William Ewart Berry (Lord
Camrose), 1879-1954: Fleet
Street 'press baron'.

Bryceson Treharne, 1880-
1948: Popular composer
and pianist in USA.

J. O. Francis, 1882-1956:
Playwright.

James Gomer Berry (Lord
Kemsley), 1883-1968: Fleet
Street 'press baron'.

Jack Jones, 1884-1970:
Popular novelist and
playwright.

Florence Smithson, 1884-1936:
Musical comedy star.

Glyn Jones, 1905-1995:
Academic and author.

David Vivian Penrose Lewis
(Lord Brecon), 1905-1976:
Conservative politician,
first Minister of State for
Welsh Affairs 1957-1964.

Arthur Davies, born 1906:
Leading geographer.

Aubrey Jones, born 1911:
Conservative and Labour
politician and businessman.

Sir Harry Llewellyn, 1911-
1999: Olympic gold
medallist, equestrianism 1952.

Bryn Jones, 1912-1985: Welsh
international footballer.

Tal Lloyd, born 1917: Senior
trade union official.

Leslie Norris, born 1921:
Noted author.

Dale Owen, 1924-1997:
Leading architect.

Eddie Thomas, 1925-1997:
Champion welterweight
boxer and manager.

Charlie Short, born 1921: Jazz
musician.

Eryl Oliver Davies, 1922-1982:
Chief Inspector of Schools
in Wales from 1972.

Leo Challaghan, born 1923:
Leading soccer referee: in
1968 only the second
Welshman ever to referee
an FA Cup Final.

Mostyn (Moss) Evans, born
1924: Senior trade unionist.

David Cole, born 1928: Leading
journalist editor 'Western
Mail' and public servant: poet.

David James, born 1929:
Educationist and public
servant.

Wyn Morris, born 1929: Leading
orchestral conductor.

Malcolm Vaughan, born 1930:
Popular singer.

Illtyd Harrington, born 1931:
Labour politician in
London and public servant.

Philip Madoc, born 1934:
Leading actor.

Howard Winstone, 1939-2000:
Champion featherweight
boxer.

Mario Basini, born 1943:
Journalist, literary editor
'Western Mail'.

William Geraint Price, born
1943: Mechanical engineer
and academic.

Kim Howells, born 1946:
Leading Labour politician:
MP for Pontypridd.

Owen Money (Lynn Mitchell),
born 1947: Popular comedian,
radio and television.

Johnny Owen, 1956-1980:
Champion bantamweight
boxer, died following a
knock-out in world title
fight in Los Angeles.

Jason Howard, born 1963:
Opera and concert baritone.

Julien Macdonald, born 1972:
Leading fashion designer.

MERTHYR VALE (Merthyr Tydfil)

Idloes Owen, 1895-1954:
Founder of Welsh National
Opera 1945-1946: choirmaster
of the Lyrian Singers from
1925.

Timothy John Evans, 1925-1950:
Hanged for the murder of
his baby daughter in London:
John Christie later confesed
to this crime and another
six murders: Evans was
pardoned in 1966.

MILFORD HAVEN (Pembrokeshire)

Arthur William Symons,
1865-1945: Poet, critic and
editor.

Sir James Frederick Rees,
1883-1967: Leading
historian and educationist.

William Lewis, 1896-1977:
Awarded the Victoria Cross
in Greece 1916.

Ted Morgan 1923-1989:
Leading educational
psychologist.

Helen Watts, born 1928:
Opera and concert soprano.

MISKIN (Rhondda Cynon Taff)

Sir Rhys Rhys-Williams, 1865-
1955: Judge and public
servant.

MOCHDRE (Conwy)

Mickey Thomas, born 1954:
Welsh international footballer.

MOCHDRE (Powys)

George Roberts, 1769-1853:
Pioneer settler in the USA.

MOLD (Flintshire)

Jane Brereton (Melissa), 1685-
1740: Poet and author.

John Blackwell (Alun), 1797-1840: Anglican minister and accomplished poet.

John Ambrose Lloyd, 1815-1874: Composer and hymnwriter.

Daniel Owen, 1836-1895: Popular Welsh-language novelist.

Hywel Hughes, 1886-1976: Wealthy rancher in Colombia: generous supporter of Welsh causes.

Huw Morris-Jones, born 1912: Academic, social theory.

MONMOUTH (Monmouthshire)

Geoffrey of Monmouth, c. 1090-1155: Writer who popularised legends of King Arthur.

Henry V, 1387-1422: Warrior king, victor of the Battle of Agincourt 1415.

Philip Evans, died 1679: Catholic priest hanged, drawn and quartered in Cardiff for treason.

Thomas Powell, 1779?-1863: Coalowner, founder of the Powell Duffryn company.

Sir Charles James Jackson, 1849-1923: Lawyer and authority on English plate.

Arthur Edwin Stevens, 1905-1995: Designer of world's first wearable electronic hearing aid, 1935: founder of Amplivox: philanthropist.

William Anthony Twiston-Davies, born 1926: President of the National Museum of Wales 1982-1987.

MONTGOMERY (Powys)

George Herbert, 1593-1633: Major poet.

Nigel Heseltine, born 1916: Poet.

MORRISTON (Swansea)

John Jones Jenkins (Lord Glantawe), 1835-1915: Tinplate magnate and public servant.

Hywel Francis Jones, born 1928: Commissioner for Local Administration (Ombudsman).

Paul Moriarty, born 1964: Welsh rugby international in both codes.

Darren Thomas, born 1975: Glamorgan cricketer.

MOSTYN (Flintshire)

Sir Herbert Williams, 1858-1933: Academic and first MP (Liberal) for the University of Wales 1918-1922.

Emlyn Williams, 1905-1987: Leading actor, author and playwright.

MOUNTAIN ASH (Rhondda Cynon Taff)

Joseph Keating, 1871-1934: Novelist.

Sir John Bailey, 1898-1969: General Secretary Co-operative Pary 1942-1967.

Philip Burton, 1904-1996: Teacher and mentor of Richard Burton (qv).

Herbert Edmund Davies (Lord), 1906-1992:

Distinguished judge: tried the Great Train Robbery case, 1964: presided at the Aberfan Tribunal 1966.

Pennar Davies, 1911-1996: Noted author.

Tom Earley, 1911-1998: Poet, pacifist and anarchist.

Emrys Jones, 1914-1991: Regional organiser, Wales Labour Party 1965-1979.

Les Manfield, born 1915: Welsh rugby international.

John Stuart Williams, born 1920: Award-winning poet.

John Darran, 1924-1997: Popular broadcaster.

Johnny Tudor, born 1945: Popular singer.

MUMBLES (Swansea)

Jim Presdee, born 1933: Glamorgan cricketer.

Ian Hislop, born 1960: Writer, editor of 'Private Eye' and broadcaster.

Catherine Zeta Jones, born 1969: Leading film actress.

MYNYDDISLWYN (Torfaen)

William Thomas (Islwyn), 1832-1878: Major poet.

N

NANMOR (Gwynedd)

Dafydd Nanmor, fl. 1450-1480: Notable poet.

NANTANOG (Anglesey)

Sir William Williams, 1634-1700: MP, Speaker of the House of Commons 1680-1684.

NANTCWNLLE (Cardiganshire)

Daniel Rowland, 1713-1790: Leading Methodist preacher.

NANTGAREDIG (Carmarthenshire)

James Eirian Davies, 1918-1998: Award-winning poet.

NANTGARW (Rhondda Cynon Taff)

Steve Fenwick born 1951: Welsh rugby international, British Lion 1977.

NANTGLYN (Denbighshire)

David Samwell, 1751-1798: Surgeon and poet: accompanied Captain Cook.

Roberts Davies, 1769-1835: Poet and early eisteddfodwr.

NANTGWYLLT (Powys)

(Now submerged beneath Caban-coch reservoir).

Emmeline Lewis Lloyd, 1827-1913: One of the first women to climb in the Alps.

NANTYFFYLLON (Bridgend)

Dave Bowen, 1928-1994: Welsh football international and Wales captain in their only World Cup Final appearance 1958.

J. J. Williams, born 1948: Welsh rugby international, British Lion 1974 and 1977.

NANTYGLO (Blaenau Gwent)

Beriah Gwynfe Evans, 1848-1927: Journalist and author: wrote the first full-length play in Welsh to be performed – 'Glyndŵr'.

John Williams 1886-1953: Awarded the Victoria Cross in France 1918.

Kingsley Jones, born 1969: Welsh rugby international.

NANTYMOEL (Bridgend)

Lyn Davies, born 1942: Olympic gold medallist, long jump 1964 and European and Commonwealth champion: Welsh Sports Personality of the Year 1964 and 1966.

NARBERTH (Penbrokeshire)

Cuthbert Collin Davies, 1896-1974: Specialist in the history of the Indian sub-continent.

Wyn Calvin, born 1927: Comedian: first Welshman to be elected King Rat of the Order of Water Rats (show business charity).

NASH (Newport)

Sir Edward Carne, c. 1500-1561: Lawyer and diplomat: acted for Henry VIII in Rome seeking divorce from Catherine of Aragon.

NEATH (Neath – Port Talbot)

Sir William Nott, 1782-1845: General: British Commander in the 1842 Afghan War.

Anna Laetitia Waring, 1823-1910: Anglican hymnwriter.

Sir Hugh Evans-Thomas, 1862-1928: Admiral: senior commander at the 1916 Battle of Jutland.

Walter Rees, 1862-1949: Secretary of the Welsh Rugby Union 1896-1948.

David (Dai) Watts-Morgan, 1867-1933: Miners' leader and Rhondda Labour MP.

Ted Hopkins, c. 1877-1937: Popular variety hall comedian.

Thomas Aubrey Leyshon (Tal) Whittington, 1881-1944: Glamorgan cricket captain.

Hugh Dalton, 1887-1962: Economist and senior Labour politician.

Glyn Stephens, 1891-1965: Welsh rugby international: President of the Welsh Rugby Union 1956-1957.

Eric Evans, 1893-1955: Secretary of the Welsh Rugby Union 1948-1955.

Maudie Edwards, 1906-1991: Popular comedienne.

Ray Milland (Reginald Truscott Jones), 1907-1986: Hollywood film star: winner of the Oscar for Best Actor 1946.

William Squire, 1920-1989: Leading actor.

Rees Stephens, 1922-1998: Welsh rugby international, British Lion 1950: son of Glyn Stephens (qv).

Thomas Henry James, born 1923: Leading Egyptologist.

Roy John, 1925-1981: Welsh rugby international, British Lion 1950.

Michael Roberts, 1927-1983: Conservative MP Cardiff North: first Head of Bishop of Llandaff School, Cardiff.

John Hughes, born 1930: Journalist, senior foreign correspondent.

Sir David Nicholls, born 1930: Journalist and television administrator.

Michael Bogdanov, born 1938: Leading stage director.

Brian Thomas, born 1940: Welsh rugby international.

Della Jones, born 1946: Opera and concert mezzo-soprano.

Clive Norling, born 1950: Leading international rugby referee.

Robert Minhinnick, born 1952: Environmentalist, poet and author.

William Alfred Thomas, born 1954: Commonwealth Games gold medallist, bowls 1986: world bronze medallist 1988.

Steve Barwick, born 1960: Glamorgan cricketer.

John Price, born 1960: World indoor bowls champion 1990.

Stuart Evans, born 1963: Welsh rugby international.

NEFYN (Gwynedd)

John Parry, 1710?-1782: Noted blind harpist and collector of Welsh airs.

Hestor Thrale, c. 1741-1821: friend and confidante of Dr Samuel Johnson.

Elizabeth Watkin Jones, 1887-1966: Children's writer.

Robert Gerallt Jones, 1934-1999: Warden of Gregynog Hall, Poet, novelist and critic.

NEVERN (Pembrokeshire)

Joshua Hughes, 1807-1889: Bishop of St Asaph.

NELSON (Caerphilly)

E. Eynon Evans, 1904-1989: Popular playwright and actor.

Sir Tudor Watkins, born 1918: Awarded the Victoria Cross in France 1944; judge and President of the Welsh Rugby Union.

Simon Weston, born 1961: Falklands War veteran, broadcaster, writer and charity worker.

NEWBRIDGE (Caerphilly)

John Dawes, born 1940: Welsh rugby international and British Lions captain 1971.

Terry Matthews, born 1944: Electronics and property tycoon, reputed to be Wales' first billionaire. Founder of Mitel and Newbridge Networks.

Helen Jenkins, 1946-1998: Journalist and senior television producer.

Rhys Harries, born 1962: Folk musician, member of 'Bwchadanas' group.

NEWCASTLE EMLYN (Cardiganshire)

Theophilus Evans, 1693-1767: Historian.

Allen Raine (Anne Adaliza Beynon Puddicombe), 1836-1908: Writer.

David Emlyn Evans, 1843-1913: Musician, composer and collector of Welsh folk tunes.

Dill Jones, 1923-1984: Noted jazz pianist.

Catrin Howell, born 1969: Artist.

NEWPORT

Francis Lewis, 1712-1802: Signatory of the 1776 American Declaration of Independence as representative of New York.

John Frost, 1784-1877: Leader of the 1839 Chartist Uprising in Newport.

John Thomas, 1829-1896: Composer of popular songs.

Horace Lyne, 1860-1949: Welsh rugby international, President of the Welsh Rugby Union 1906-1947.

Tom Baker Jones, 1862-1959: Welsh rugby international, scorer of Wales's first international try, Dublin 1882.

Arthur (Monkey) Gould, 1864-1919: Welsh rugby international.

W. H. Davies, 1871-1940: Acclaimed poet.

James Henry (Jimmy) Thomas, 1874-1949: Railwaymen's leader and senior Labour politician.

Bertie Pardoe Thomas, 1877-1937: Leading Newport shipowner.

George Travers, 1877-1945: Welsh rugby international.

Ellis Lloyd, 1879-1939: Journalist, lawyer, novelist and Labour MP.

Tommy Vile, 1882-1958: Welsh rugby international and British Lion 1904.

Walter Griffiths, 1884-1938: Railwaymen's leader.

Reg Plummer, 1888-1953: Welsh rugby international and British Lion 1910.

Harold Tilney, 1888-1948: South Wales pioneer owner of cinema chain.

Mai Jones, 1899-1960: BBC radio producer and joint composer of 'We'll Keep a Welcome'.

Harold Edwards, 1900-1989: Distinguished surgeon.

Bill Everson, 1905-1966: Welsh rugby international and administrator.

John Linton, 1905-1943: Awarded the Victoria Cross posthumously off Corsica on submarine HMS 'Turbulent'.

Melbourne Thomas, 1906-1989: First Chief Constable South Wales Police 1969.

Raymond Glendenning, 1907-1974: Radio and television sports commentator.

John Evans, 1911-1943: Welsh rugby international: captain in his one game.

William (Bunner) Travers, born 1913: Welsh rugby international, British Lion 1938: son of George Travers (qv).

Desmond Llywelyn, 1914-2000: Actor, noted for playing 'Q' in James Bond films.

Eric Thomas, 1914-1998: Leading physical education instructor.

Johnny Morris, 1917-1999: Television animal programmes presenter.

Alison Bielski, born 1925: Poet.

John Brockway, born 1929: Commonwealth Games gold medallist, swimming 1954.

Trevor Brewer, born 1930: Welsh rugby international and athlete.

Leslie Thomas, born 1931: Popular novelist and broadcaster.

Keith Baxter, born 1933: Actor and playwright.

Glyn Davidge, born 1933: Welsh rugby international.

Kenneth Baker, born 1934: Leading Conservative politician.

Rex Richards, 1934-1987: Welsh rugby international and water shows diver.

Dick Richardson, 1934-1999: Champion heavyweight boxer.

John Humphries, born 1937: Journalist, editor of the 'Western Mail'.

Brian Flook, born 1940: Champion swimmer.

Suart Watkins, born 1941: Welsh rugby international British Lion 1966.

Bobbie Windsor, born 1946: Welsh rugby international, British Lion 1974 and 1977.

Nick Evans, born 1947: Jazz trombonist.

Keith Jarrett, born 1948: Welsh rugby international.

David Burcher, born 1950: Welsh rugby international, British Lion 1977.

David Pearce, 1951-2000: British heavyweight boxing champion.

Eddie Butler, born 1957: Welsh rugby international, British Lion 1983 and television sports presenter.

Debbie Johnsey, born 1957: Leading equestrian competitor.

Peter Nicholas, born 1959: Welsh football international.

Robert Clift, born 1962: Olympic gold medallist, hockey 1988.

Andrew Davies, born 1967: Commonwealth Games medallist, weightlifting, gold 1990, bronze 1986.

Michael Sheen, born 1969: Actor.

Nathan Blake, born 1972: Welsh football internationl.

Christian Malcolm, born 1979: Commonwealth Games silver medallist, 200 metres 1998.

NEWPORT (Pembrokeshire)

Dillwyn Miles, born 1916: Gorsedd Herald Bard and author.

NEW QUAY (Cardiganshire)

David Emrys James (Dewi Emrys), 1881-1952: Poet, winner of National Eisteddfod Chair 1929, 1930, 1943 and 1948 and Crown 1926.

NEWTOWN (Powys)

Robert Owen, 1771-1858: Factory owner, socialist, trade unionist and co-operative movement pioneer.

John Basson Humphrey, 1824-1891: Goldminers' leader in Victoria, Australia, and first Minister of Mines there.

Sir Pryce Pryce-Jones, 1834-1920: Mill owner and mail order pioneer.

Albert Howard Trow, 1863-1939: Botanist and academic: Principal University College, Cardiff, 1919-1929.

Eiluned Lewis, 1900-1979: Poet, novelist and journalist.

Glyn Tegai Hughes, born 1923: Gregynog Hall warden: television administrator.

NEW TREDEGAR (Caerphilly)

Leighton Jenkins, born 1931: Welsh rugby international.

NEYLAND (Pembrokeshire)

Gordon Samuel Parry (Lord), born 1925: Businessman and public servant.

NORTH CORNELLY (Bridgend)

Owen Teale, born 1961: Actor: winner of Broadway Tony for Best Featured Actor 1997.

John Humphries, born 1969: Welsh rugby international, British Lion 1997.

NORTHOP (Flintshire)

William Parry, died 1585: Executed for his part in a plot to assassinate Elizabeth I.

Edith Wynne, 1840-1897: Singer and actress known as 'the Welsh nightingale'.

O

OGMORE VALE (Bridgend)

Dorothy Edwards, 1903-1934: Novelist and short story writer.

Grahame Hodgson, born 1936: Welsh rugby international.

ONLLWYN (Neath – Port Talbot)

Dai Francis, 1911-1981: Miners' leader: prominent South Wales Communist.

Hywel Francis, born 1946: Historian, educationist and author: son of the above, Labour MP for Aberavon.

OYSTERMOUTH (Swansea)

Alice Matilda Langland Williams (Alis Mallt Williams), 1867-1950: Novelist.

P

PANDY (Monmouthshire)
Raymond Williams, 1921-1985:
Literary critic and novelist.

PEMBROKE (Pembrokeshire)
Henry Tudor, 1457-1509: The
first Tudor king following
his victory at the Battle of
Bosworth, Leicestershire, 1485.
Mervyn Johns, 1899-1992:
Popular stage and screen
actor.
William Grimes, 1905-1988:
Leading archaeologist.
Daniel Jones, 1912-1993:
Distinguished composer.
Carl Llewellyn, born 1965:
Grand National winning
jockey 1992 and 1998.

**PEMBROKE DOCK
(Pembrokeshire)**
John Harper Narbeth, 1863-
1944: Naval architect, pioneer
of aircraft carrier design.
Thomas George John, 1880-
1946: Founder of Alvis
sports car company.
William John Abbott Davies,
1890-1967: English rugby
international: team captain.
Jamie Owen, born 1968:
Television presenter.

PENARTH (Vale of Glamorgan)
Sir David Duncan, 1847-1923:
Proprietor of the 'South Wales
Echo'.

Robert Ithel Treharne Rees,
1881-1946: President of
South Wales Institute of
Engineers.
Richard Wain, 1896-1917:
Awarded the Victoria Cross
posthumously in France.
Sir Henry Lewis Guy, 1887-
1956: Distinguished
mechanical engineer.
Samuel Pearse, 1897-1919:
Awarded the Victoria Cross
posthumously in Russia.
Eric Linklater, 1899-1974:
Distinguished writer.
Kathleen Thomas, born 1906:
In 1927, the first person to
swim the Bristol Channel –
Penarth to Weston.
Haydn Harold Jones, born 1920:
Senior churchman, Bishop
of Venezuela 1976-1981.
Kenyon Emrys-Roberts, 1923-
1998: Composer of music
for films and television.
Peter Temple-Morris, born
1938: Conservative and
Labour politician.
David Sullivan, born 1949:
Millionaire publisher and
football club owner.

PENBOYR (Carmarthenshire)
Griffith Jones, 1683-1761:
Vicar of Llanddowror:
originator of the circulating
schools movement.

PENBRYN (Cardiganshire)
John Geraint Jenkins, born
1929: Folk historian.

PENCARN (Monmouthshire)
Sir Thomas Morgan, c. 1542-
1595: Distinguished soldier.

PENCLAWDD (Swansea)
Karl Jenkins, born 1944: Film
music composer.

PENCOED (Bridgend)
Evan Davies (Myfyr
Morganwg), 1801-1888:
Poet, claimant to the title of
'Archdruid'.

PENDERYN (Bridgend)
Richard Lewis (Dic
Penderyn), 1808-1831:
Wales's 'first working class
martyr', hanged in Cardiff
for his alleged part in the
1831 Merthyr Rising.

PENDERYN (Rhondda Cynon Taff)
John Jones (Shoni Sgubor
Fawr), 1811-1858:
Transported to Australia as
a Rebecca rioter in 1843.
Richard Bell, 1859-1930:
Railworkers' leader involved
in the historic Taff Vale
Railway strike 1900: Labour
MP.

PENDOYLAN (Vale of Glamorgan)
Thomas William, 1761-1844:
Hymnwriter.

PENLEY (Flintshire)
Dick Krzywicki, born 1947:
Welsh international
footballer.

PENLLERGAER (Swansea)
John Dilwyn-Llewellyn, 1810-
1882: Experimental scientist,
pioneer photographer,
Fellow of the Royal Society.

PENMACHNO (Gwynedd)
William Morgan, 1541?-1604:
Bishop, translator of the
Bible into Welsh published
in 1588.

PENMAENMAWR (Gwynedd)
Edward Gwylfa Roberts,
1871-1935: Congregational
minister and poet, winner
of the National Eisteddfod
Crown 1898 and 1899.
Sir Wynne Cemlyn-Jones,
1883-1966: Barrister, Liberal
politician and public servant.

PENMON (Vale of Glamorgan)
Edward Williams (Iolo
Morganwg), 1747-1826:
Poet, forger, incurable
romantic: founder of the
Gorsedd.

PENMORFA (Gwynedd)
John Thomas (Eifionydd),
1848-1922: Journalist, editor
and founder of 'Y Genhinen'
literary magazine.

PENNAL (Powys)

Arthur Lascelles, 1880-1918: Awarded the Victoria Cross in France 1917.

Ian Hamilton Burton, born 1918: Archimandrite of the Greek Orthodox Church.

PEN-PONT (Powys)

Dafydd Gam (Dafydd ap Llywelyn), died 1415: Soldier, once a prisoner of Owain Glyndŵr, killed at the Battle of Agincourt: reputed to be the Welshman on whom Shakespeare based Fluellen in his 'Henry V'.

PENRHIWCEIBER (Rhondda Cynon Taff)

George Hall (Viscount), 1881-1965: Senior Labour politician and public servant.

Arthur Lloyd James, 1884-1943: Phonetician.

Frank Llywelyn Jones, born 1907: Physicist.

Robert Morgan, born 1921: Poet.

Bryn Campbell, born 1933: Leading press photographer and picture editor.

PENRHOS (Monmouthshire)

Sir Roger Williams, 1549?-1595: Distinguished soldier.

PENRHOS (Powys)

Rowland Ellis, 1656-1731: Quaker emigrant to Pennsylvania after whose farm there Bryn Mawr College is named.

PENRHYNDEUDRAETH (Gwynedd)

Humphrey Humphries, 1648-1712: Antiquarian whose researches assisted Edward Lhuyd (qv).

PENRHYNGOCH (Cardiganshire)

Dafydd ap Gwilym, c. 1320-c. 1370: Wales's foremost medieval poet.

PENSARN (Anglesey)

Lewis William Lewis, 1831-1901: Poet and novelist.

PENTIR (Gwynedd)

Noreen Louisa Edwards, born 1926: Senior medical administrator.

PENTRE (Rhondda Cynon Taff)

Ellen Evans, 1891-1953: Principal, Glamorgan Training College, Barry, 1923: Welsh language teaching pioneer.

Sydney Tapper-Jones, 1904-1991: Solicitor and Cardiff Town Clerk 1942-1970.

Jimmy Murphy, born 1910: Welsh football international and team manager in Wales's only World Cup Final appearance 1958.

Rhydwen Williams, 1916-1997: Novelist and poet: winner of the National Eisteddfod Crown 1946 and 1964.

Sir Ray Powell, born 1928: Labour MP for Ogmore.

PENTRE-POETH (Swansea)

John Viriamu Jones, 1856-
1901: Educationist and
academic: first Principal of
University College, Cardiff.

PENUWCH (Cardiganshire)

John Frederick Rees, born 1920:
Poet, winner of the National
Eisteddfod Crown 1984 and
1985.

PEN-Y-BANC (Cardiganshire)

Lewis Edwards, 1809-1887:
Principal of Bala Calvinistic
Methodist College for its
first fifty years.

PEN-Y-BERTH (Gwynedd)

Robert Gwyn, 1540-c. 1592:
Major theological writer.

PENYGOES (Powys)

Richard Wilson, 1714-1781:
Distinguished landscape
painter.

PENYGRAIG (Rhondda Cynon Taff)

Tom Thomas, 1880-1911:
British middleweight
boxing champion.
Sir Clifford Morgan, 1901-
1986: Leading surgeon.
Gareth Griffiths, born 1931:
Welsh rugby international,
British Lion 1955.

PENYGROES (Carmarthenshire)

Daniel Powell Williams
(Pastor Dan), 1882-1947:
Founder and first President
of the Apostolic Church.

PENYGROES (Gwynedd)

Llyfni Huws, 1889-1962:
Harpist and penillion
performer.
Bryn Terfel, born 1965:
Internationally famous opera
and concert baritone: first
winner of the Cardiff Singer
of the World lieder prize 1989.

PICTON CASTLE (Pembrokeshire)

Sir John Philips, 1666-1737:
MP and religious reformer
active in the Society for the
Promotion of Christian
Knowledge.

PILLETH (Powys)

Charles Price, died 1646:
Royalist soldier, campaigned
in Ireland, killed in a duel.

PONTARDAWE (Swansea)

Ben Davies, 1858-1943: Noted
tenor.
David James Jones (Gwenallt),
1899-1968: Poet, winner of
the National Eisteddfod
Chair 1926 and 1931.
Garnet Rees, 1912-1990:
French language scholar.
Ronnie James, born 1917:
Champion lightweight boxer.
Dafydd Rowlands, born 1931:
Writer and poet: winner of
National Eisteddfod Crown
1969 and 1971; Archdruid
of Wales 1996-1999.
Mary Hopkin, born 1950:
Popular singer.

71

PONTARDDULAIS
(Carmarthenshire)
Sir Evans Williams, 1871-1959: Leading coalowner: Chair of the Coalowners' Association.

T. Gunstone Jones, 1893-1951: Popular actor.

Rhydwen Harding Evans, 1900-1993: Civil engineer.

Ron Mathias, 1912-1968: Senior trade unionist and public servant.

Dennis O'Neill, born 1948: Leading operatic tenor.

Derwyn Jones, born 1970: Welsh rugby international.

PONTERWYD (Cardiganshire)
Sir John Rhys, 1840-1915: Distinguished philologist: first Professor of Celtic at Oxford University.

Geraint Howells (Lord), 1925-1995: Liberal MP.

PONTLEPOIR
(Pembrokeshire)
Desmond Davies, born 1958: Commonwealth Games gold medallist, shooting 1998.

PONTLLANFRAITH
(Caerphilly)
Roy Hughes (Lord Hughes of Casnewydd), born 1925: Labour MP.

PONTLOTTYN (Caerphilly)
Edmund William Stonelake, 1873-1960: Labour Party politician and pioneer socialist.

Edward Thomas Chapman, born 1920: Awarded the Victoria Cross in Germany 1945.

PONT NEATH VAUGHAN
(Powys)
Thomas Stephens, 1824-1875: Literary critic: demolisher of the Madoc legend.

PONTNEWYDD (Torfaen)
Fred Parfitt, 1869-1953: Welsh rugby international.

Sir Thomas Jones, 1881-1948: Senior civil servant: authority on food distribution and rationing.

PONTNEWYNYDD (Torfaen)
Sir John Ballinger, 1860-1933: First Librarian National Library of Wales.

Myfanwy Haycock, 1913-1963: Poet.

Bryn Meredith, born 1930: Welsh rugby international, British Lion 1955, 1959 and 1962: Welsh Sports Personality of the Year 1961.

Dame Gwyneth Jones, born 1936: Leading operatic soprano.

PONTRHYDFENDIGAID
(Cardiganshire)
Lyn Ebenezer, born 1939: Journalist, author and broadcaster.

PONTRHYDYFEN (Neath – Port Talbot)
Brinley Thomas, 1906-1994: Leading economist.

72

Richard Burton (Jenkins), 1925-1984: Renowned stage and screen actor.

Ivor Emmanuel, born 1926: Popular singer: star of long-running network television show 'Land of Song'.

Rebecca Evans, born 1963: Opera and concert soprano.

PONTROBERT (Powys)

John Davies, 1771-1855: Early missionary to Tahiti.

Dyddgu Owen, 1906-1992: Children's writer.

PONTYBEREM (Carmarthenshire)

Dorothy Squires, 1915-1998: Popular singing star.

PONTYCYMMER (Bridgend)

Sir Daniel Davies, 1899-1966: Royal physician.

Edwin (Ted) Greenslade, 1911-1977: Garw Valley miner who set a record for cutting and loading coal in 1947.

John Lloyd, born 1943: Welsh rugby international.

John Devereux, born 1966: Welsh rugby international, British Lion 1989.

PONTYPOOL (Torfaen)

Sir Charles Hanbury Williams, 1708-1759: Satirist and diplomat: British ambassador to Russia.

Morgan Edwards, 1722-1795: Co-founder of Brown University, Rhode Island.

Thomas Henry Thomas, 1839-1915: Artist: founder member of the Royal Cambrian Academy, Conwy 1881.

Cliff Pritchard, 1881-1954: Welsh rugby international.

Arthur D. K. Owen, 1904-1970: Senior United Nations official 1945-1965.

Ray Prosser, born 1927: Welsh rugby international, British Lion 1959.

Allan Lewis, born 1942: Welsh rugby international, British Lion 1966.

PONTYPRIDD (Rhondda Cynon Taff)

Edward Thomas John, 1857-1931: Industrialist, Liberal MP and Welsh home rule supporter.

David Thomas Oliver, 1863-1947: Academic lawyer.

Christopher Jones, 1886-1937: Olympic gold medallist, water polo 1920.

Freddie Welsh (Frederick Hall Thomas), 1886-1927: Champion lightweight boxer, world title holder 1914-1917.

Robert Bye, 1889-1962: Awarded the Victoria Cross in France 1917.

Arthur Pearson, 1897-1980: Labour MP for Pontypridd.

Geraint Dyfnallt Owen, 1908-1993: Historian and novelist.

Harry Rees, 1908-1978: Welsh rugby international.

Gethyn Stoodley Thomas, 1913-1997: Writer and BBC producer.

Desmond Brayley (Lord), 1917-1977: Millionaire industrialist, socialist and public servant.

J. B. G. (Bryn) Thomas, 1917-1997: Sports journalist and author: brother of Gethyn Stoodley.

Elaine Morgan, born 1920: Author and playwright.

John Gwilliam, born 1923: Welsh rugby international.

Bernard Hedges, born 1927: Glamorgan cricketer.

Jenny Jones, born 1927: Bristol Channel swimmer 1949 and 1950: in 1951 first Welsh person to swim the English Channel.

Alun Richards, born 1929: Novelist and playwright.

Bryn Williams, born 1931: Popular singer and entertainer.

Russell Robbins, born 1932: Welsh rugby international, British Lion 1955.

David Parry-Jones, born 1933: Broadcaster, journalist and author.

John Hughes, born 1934: Potter, noted for his 'Grogs' creations.

Brynmor John, 1934-1989: Labour MP for Pontypridd.

Wayne Chandler, born 1935: Jazz musician.

Kingsley Jones, born 1935: Welsh rugby international, British Lion 1962.

Geraint Stanley Jones, born 1936: Controller BBC Wales 1981-1985.

John L. Hughes, born 1938: Novelist.

Tom Davies, born 1941: Novelist and journalist.

Iris Williams, born 1945: Popular singing star.

Terry Jones, born 1946: Leading darts player.

Tom David, born 1948: Welsh rugby international and British Lion 1974.

Neil Jenkins, born 1971: Welsh rugby international and British Lion 1997 and 2001.

Neil Swain, born 1971: Champion super-bantamweight boxer.

Lee Jarvis, born 1976: Welsh rugby international.

PONTYWAUN (Caerphilly)

Vernon Hartshorn, 1872-1931: Cabinet minister in the first Labour government 1924.

Jeff Squire, born 1951: Welsh rugby international, British Lion 1977, 1980 and 1983.

PORTH (Rhondda Cynon Taff)

Noah Ablett, 1883-1935: Militant miners' leader.

Percy Jones, 1895-1922: Champion featherweight boxer, world champion 1914.

Iforwyn Glyndwr Davies, 1901-1984: Authority on public health.

John Gwyn Griffiths, born 1911: Award-winning poet: husband of Kate Bosse-Griffiths, father of Heini and Robat Gruffudd (qv).

Cliff Jones, 1914-1990: Welsh rugby international: President Welsh Rugby Union 1980-1981.

Geraint Jones, 1917-1998: Organist and conductor.

Gordon Wells, 1928-1996: Welsh rugby international.

PORT DINORWIC (Y FELINHELI (Gwynedd)

Meirion Edwards, born 1940: Head of BBC Radio Cymru 1980.

PORT EYNON (Swansea)

Don Shepherd, born 1927: Glamorgan cricketer.

PORTHCAWL (Bridgend)

Robert Glenton, 1920-1978: Leading Fleet Street journalist.

Ted Rowlands, born 1940: Senior Labour MP.

Clive Williams, born 1948: Welsh rugby international, British Lion 1977 and 1980.

Jason Hughes, born 1971: Actor.

PORTHMADOG (Gwynedd)

David Owen (Dafydd y Garreg Wen), 1720-1749: Renowned harpist.

Eliseus Williams (Eifion Wyn), 1867-1926: Poet.

Gwyn Jones, born 1948: Business innovator, Chair of Welsh Development Agency.

Tom Whitaker, born 1949: In 1998, the first amputee to reach the summit of Mount Everest.

Siân Brice, born 1969: Leading triathlete.

PORT TALBOT (Neath – Port Talbot)

Gwyn Williams, 1904-1990: Critic and poet.

Llywellyn Heycock (Lord), 1905-1990: Labour politician and educationist; Chair Glamorgan County Council.

David Philip Evans, 1908-1995: Educationist, first Principal Glamorgan Polytechnic.

Roland Oliver Fenton (Ronald Welch), 1909-1982: Novelist.

George Thomas (Viscount Tonypandy), 1909-1997: Labour politician: Secretary of State for Wales, Speaker of the House of Commons and leading Methodist layman.

Vivian Jenkins, born 1911: Welsh rugby international, British Lion 1938 and sports correspondent.

Moelwyn Merchant, 1913-1997: Poet and critic.

Tom Jenkins, born 1920: Leading trade unionist.

Geoffrey Howe (Lord), born 1926: Senior Conservative politician: Chancellor of the Exchequer and Foreign Secretary.

Clive Jenkins, born 1926-1999: Leading trade unionist.

Freddie Williams, born 1926: World speedway champion 1950 and 1958.

Ronald Lewis, 1928-1982: Stage and screen actor.

Illtyd Rhys Lloyd, born 1929:
Educationist, Chief
Inspector of Schools, 1982.

Andrew Vicari, born 1938:
Noted artist.

Alan Durban, born 1941:
Welsh football international.

Clayton Heycock, born 1941:
Secretary, Welsh Joint
Education Committee, 1990:
son of Lord Heycock (qv).

Ray Rees, born 1943: Economist.

Allan Martin, born 1948:
Welsh rugby international,
British Lion 1977 and 1980.

Brian Flynn, born 1955: Welsh
football international.

Christopher Evans, born 1959:
Millionaire biotechnologist.

POYSTON (Pembrokeshire)

Sir Thomas Picton, 1758-1815:
general, killed at the Battle
of Waterloo.

PRESTATYN (Denbighshire)

Gordon Macdonald (Lord),
1888-1966: Labour politician:
last Governor General of
independent Newfoundland.

Emyr Humphries, born 1919:
Award-winning novelist.

Peggy Cummins, born 1925:
Leading stage and screen
actress.

John Prescott, born 1938:
Senior Labour politician:
Deputy Prime Minister.

Gareth Wyn Williams (Lord),
born 1941: Leading
barrister and judge.

John Desmond Prescott Thomas,
born 1942: Television executive
and public servant.

Carol Vorderman, born 1960:
Television presenter.

PUNCHESTON (Pembrokeshire)

Evan Rees (Dyfed), 1850-1923:
Poet, winner of National
Eisteddfod Chair 1881, 1884,
1889 and 1901: Archdruid
of Wales 1905-1923.

PWLLHELI (Gwynedd)

John Elias, 1774-1841:
Methodist leader.

Eleazer Roberts, 1825-1912:
Tonic Sol-fa method of
music teaching pioneer.

Thomas Owen Jones, 1875-
1941: Librarian, dramatist
and actor.

Sir William Davies, 1887-
1952: Librarian, National
Library of Wales.

Sir Albert Evans-Jones (Cynan),
1895-1970: Poet, winner of
the National Eisteddfod
Chair 1921, 1923 and 1931
and Crown 1924; the only
person to have served as
Archdruid of Wales twice,
1950-1954 and 1963-1966.

John Robert Jones, 1911-1970:
Philosopher, writer on
Welsh identity.

Thomas Owen Prichard, born
1932: Environmentalist and
ecologist.

Endaf Emlyn, born 1944: Film
director.

PYLE (Bridgend)

Howell Davies, born 1959: Welsh
rugby international.

Q

QUAKERS YARD (Merthyr Tydfil)
David Morgan, executed 1746: Barrister and Jacobite, captured after the 1745 rebellion.

Jimmy Wilde, 1892-1969: Champion flyweight boxer, world title holder 1916-1923.

R

RAGLAN (Monmouthshire)
William Gunter, executed 1588: Catholic priest hanged in London for heresy.
Robert Jones, 1857-1898: Awarded the Victoria Cross at Rorke's Drift, South Africa 1879

RESOLVEN (Neath – Port Talbot)
David Evans, 1874-1948: Composer and editor of 'Y Cerddor' 1916-1931.
Thomas Hopkin Evans, 1879-1940: Organist, conductor and author.
Michael Barry, born 1942: Television chef.

RHAYADER (Powys)
Thomas Jones, 1819-1892: Poet, preacher, leading Congregationalist.

RHIGOS (Rhondda Cynon Taff)
Maldwyn Thomas Davies, born 1950: Opera and concert singer.
Glyn Shaw, born 1951: Welsh rugby international.

RHOSGADFAN (Gwynedd)
Kate Roberts, 1891-1971: Distinguished novelist.

RHOSILI (Swansea)
Edgar Evans, 1876-1912: Royal Navy petty officer who died on Scott's South Pole expedition.

RHOSLLANERCHRUGOG (Wrexham)
William Davies, 1859-1907: Musician with senior positions at Magdalen College, Oxford, and St Paul's Cathedral.

Sir Brynmor Jones, 1903-1989: Chemist, educationist and public servant.

Gwilym Bowyer, 1906-1965: Theologian, broadcaster and pacifist.

Tom Jones, 1908-1990: International Brigader in Spanish Civil War: founder member of Wales TUC.

Arwel Hughes, 1908-1988: Composer and conductor: Head of Music BBC Wales: father of Owain Arwel Hughes (qv).

Meredith Edwards, 1917-1999: Popular and successful actor.

Raymond Edwards, 1919-1999: Principal Welsh College of Music and Drama, Cardiff 1959-1984.

Glyn Phillips, born 1927: Chemist and educationist.

Mark Hughes, born 1963: Welsh football international.

RHOS-ON-SEA (Conwy)

Wilfred Wooller, 1912-1997: Welsh rugby international, Glamorgan cricket captain and England cricket selector.

RHOSTYLLEN (Wrexham)

Charles Edward Gittins, 1908-1970: Leading educationist.

RHUDDLAN (Denbighshire)

Sir Ernest Jones-Parry, 1908-1998: Historian and civil servant.

Philip Jones Griffiths, born 1936: Photojournalist noted for his coverage of the 1970s Vietnam War.

RHYD-DDU (Gwynedd)

Sir Thomas Parry-Williams, 1887-1975: Poet and scholar: in 1912 the first person to win both Chair and Crown at a National Eisteddfod, a feat he repeated in 1915.

RHYDLEWIS (Cardiganshire)

Elizabeth Mary Jones, 1878-1953: Novelist.

RHYDYCYMERAU (Carmarthenshire)

David John Williams, 1885-1970: Writer and nationalist: jailed for his part in the 1936 Pen-y-berth arson incident.

RHYDYFELIN (Cardiganshire)

Richard Jones, born 1926: Award-winning novelist.

RHYL (Denbighshire)

Sir Robert Jones, 1858-1933: Leading orthopaedic surgeon.

William Hughes Jones, 1885-1951: Literary critic.

Albert Gubay, born 1929: Millionaire founder of Kwiksave Stores.

Ruth Ellis, 1927-1955: The last woman to be hanged in Britain.

Neris Hughes, born 1941: Popular actress.

John Griffiths, born 1949: Journalist, editor of the 'Liverpool Echo'.

Lee Evans, born 1964: Comedian and actor.

RHYMNEY (Caerphilly)

Thomas Jones, 1870-1955: Educationist and senior civil servant.

Idris Davies, 1905-1953: Noted poet.

Gerallt Jones, 1907-1984: Poet.

Thomas Ieuan Jeffreys-Jones, 1909-1967: Warden of Coleg Harlech.

Zoe Cresswell, 1916-1992: Popular soprano.

RISCA (Caerphilly)

William Brace, 1865-1947: Miners' leader.

Sir Charles Edwards, 1867-1954: Miners' official and Labour MP.

Tom Richards, born 1910: Olympic silver medallist, Marathon 1948.

Bill Tamplin, 1917-1989: Welsh rugby international.

ROCH CASTLE (Pembrokeshire)

Lucy Walter, 1630?-1658: Mistress to Charles II and mother of the ill-fated Duke of Monmouth.

ROGERSTONE (Newport)

William Herbert Vaughan, 1894-1959: Chair, Welsh Land Settlement Society and public servant.

Stephen Jones, born 1953: Chief rugby correspondent 'Sunday Times'.

ROSEMARKET (Pembrokeshire)

Ann Williams, 1706-1783: Poet and friend of Dr Samuel Johnson.

ROSSETT (Denbighshire)

Darwell Stone, 1859-1941: Prominent Anglo-Catholic theologian.

Alex Carlile, born 1948: Leading Liberal Democrat politician.

ROWEN (Gwynedd)

Huw T. Edwards, 1892-1970: Labour and Plaid Cymru activist: Chair of Council for Wales 1948-1958.

Dafydd Parri, born 1926: Children's writer.

RUABON (Wrexham)

John ap John, 1625?-1697: Leading Quaker.

Samuel Evans, 1859-1935: Administrator in Egyptian Coast Guard Service and Johannesburg gold mining.

Miles Thomas (Lord), 1897-1980: Military aviator: Chair of British Overseas Airways Corporation and the Development Corporation for Wales.

James Idwal Jones, 1900-1988: Geographer and Labour MP.

Will Roberts, 1907-2000: Noted painter.

Thomas Somerville Roberts, born 1911: Transport expert and public servant.

RUDRY (Caerphilly)
William Price, 1800-1893: Self-styled druid, Chartist, radical and cremation pioneer.

RUTHIN (Denbighshire)
Edward Pugh, c. 1761-1813: Artist.

John Daniel Jones, 1865-1942: Leading Congregationalist/Free Church minister and author.

Don Dale-Jones, born 1935: Editor and critic.

Tom Pryce, 1949-1977: racing driver killed in practice for South African Grand Prix.

S

ST ASAPH (Denbighshire)
Siôn Tudur, c. 1522-1602: One of the last poets patronised by the Welsh gentry: one-time member of both the Yeomen of the Guard and the Yeomen of the Crown.

William Williams, 1832-1900: Leading veterinary surgeon.

Felix Powell, born 1878, death not traced: Wrote the music of 'Pack Up Your Troubles In Your Old Kitbag', World War One popular song.

Ian Rush, born 1961: Welsh football international: first Welshman to win the European Golden Boot Award, 1984: Welsh Sports Personality of the Year 1984.

Barry Horne, born 1962: Welsh football international.

Ian Shaw, born 1962: Jazz pianist and singer.

ST ATHAN (Vale of Glamorgan)
Mark Mouland, born 1961: Leading golfer.

ST BRIDE'S BAY (Pembrokeshire)
St David, c. 515-589: Patron saint of Wales.

ST BRIDE'S MAJOR (Vale of Glamorgan)
Iorwerth Fynglwyd, fl. 1485-1527: Praise poet of the gentry, especially in the Vale of Glamorgan.

ST BRIDE'S WENTLOOG (Newport)
Lyn Harding, 1867-1952: Leading stage and film actor.

ST CLEARS (Pembrokeshire)
Thomas Charles, 1755-1814: Early Methodist leader.

Thomas Shankland, 1858-1927: Outstanding librarian at University College, Bangor.

Beti Hughes, 1926-1981: Novelist.

ST DAVID'S (Pembrokeshire)

Thomas Tomkins II, 1572-1656: Highly regarded composer.

Richard Fenton, 1747-1821: Antiquarian: topographical writer on Pembrokeshire and Wales.

Richard Llywellyn, 1906-1983: Novelist, 'How Green Was My Valley' by far his most successful book.

James Nicholas (Jâms Nicholas), born 1928: Poet, winner of National Eisteddfod Chair 1969, Archdruid of Wales 1981-1984.

Rowland Phillips, born 1956: Welsh rugby international in both codes.

ST DOGWELLS (Pembrokeshire)

William Davies Evans, 1790-1872: Inventor of the Evans Gambit move in chess.

ST DONAT'S (Vale of Glamorgan)

Sir Edward Stradling, 1529-1609: Builder of wall and harbour at St Donat's.

ST FAGANS (Cardiff)

William Miles, 1812-1902: Coalowner, property developer and banker in the USA.

Sir Edgeworth David, 1858-1934: Geologist, leader of the first party to reach the Magnetic South Pole 1909: found the coal deposits at Newcastle, New South Wales 1886.

ST NICHOLAS (Vale of Glamorgan)

Rice Merrick, c. 1520-1587: Historian and genealogist.

Sir Thomas Button, died 1634: Sailor and Arctic explorer: Button Island, Hudson Bay, is named after him.

Sir Clifford Cory, 1859-1940: Coalowner and industrialist.

SARN (Bridgend)

Kevin Fergus Sinnott, born 1947: Noted painter.

SAUNDERSFOOT (Pembrokeshire)

Bill Frost, 1848-1935: Inventor, may have been the first man to fly seven years before the Wright brothers.

SARNAU (Gwynedd)

Gerallt Lloyd Owen, born 1944: Award-winning poet.

Iwan Bala, born 1956: Prominent artist.

SEBASTOPOL (Torfaen)

George Lewis, 1908-1956: Glamorgan cricketer and coach.

SENGHENYDD (Caerphilly)

Ifor Bach (Ifor ap Meurig), fl. later twelfth century: Welsh

ruler famed for kidnapping
Earl and Countess of
Gloucester from Cardiff
Castle 1158.

SEVEN SISTERS (Neath – Port Talbot)

Ruth Bidgood, born 1922:
Award-winning poet.
Phil Davies, born 1963: Welsh
rugby international.

SHOTTON (Flintshire)

Henry Weale, 1897-1959:
Awarded the Victoria Cross
in France 1918.
Syd Lawrence 1924-1998:
Popular dance band leader.

SHIRENEWTON (Monmouthshire)

Bill Benjamin, 1824-1906:
Champion bare-knuckles
prize fighter.

SIRHOWY (Blaenau Gwent)

Ebenezer Rees, 1848-1908:
Printer and publisher.
Oliver Harris, 1873-1944:
Miners' leader.

SKEWEN (Neath – Port Talbot)

Sir Samuel Evans, 1859-1918:
Leading lawyer.
Thomas Mardy Rees, 1871-1953:
Minister, author and historian.
David de Lloyd, 1883-1948:
Composer and educationist:
first music graduate of the
University of Wales.
Bonnie Tyler, born 1953:
Popular singer.

SLEBECH (Pembrokeshire)

Roger Barlow, fl. early sixteenth
century: Sailor and writer.
Augustus Anson, 1835-1877:
Awarded the Victoria Cross
during the Indian Mutiny
1857.

SOLVA (Pembrokeshire)

Mike Stevens, born 1942:
Singer/songwriter and poet.

STAYLITTLE (Powys)

Sir David Brunt, 1886-1965:
Leading meteorologist.

STRATA FLORIDA (Cardiganshire)

William Tudur Jones, 1865-
1946: Philosopher, author
and editor.

SWANSEA

Calvert Richard Jones, 1802-
1877: Photographic pioneer
and artist.
Thomas William, 1818-1865:
Medical practioner and
scientist.
Henry Hussey Vivian (first
Baron Swansea) 1821-1894:
Copper baron.
Elizabeth Amy Dillwyn, 1845-
1935: Businesswoman and
writer.
Howell Arthur Gwynne,
1865-1950: Leading London
journalist.
David Williams, 1865-1940:
Labour MP: first Labour
Mayor of Swansea 1912-1913:
Co-operative movement
leader.

James James, c. 1866-1929: Welsh rugby international.

Evans James, c. 1869-1901: Welsh rugby international, brother of James.

W. J. Bancroft, 1871-1959: Welsh rugby international.

William John Trew, 1878-1926: Welsh rugby international.

William John Williams, 1878-1952: Educationist and public servant.

Jack Bancroft, 1879-1942: Welsh rugby international, brother of W. J.

David (Dai) Grenfell, 1881-1968: Labour MP.

David Joseph, 1883-1959: Coalowner: established Coney Beach fairground Porthcawl 1921.

Sir Llewellyn Thomas Gorton Soulsby, 1885-1966: Naval architect involved with Bristol Channel ship repairing.

Sir Lincoln Evans, 1889-1970: Trade union leader: General Secretary steelworkers' union (ISTC), 1946-1953.

Stan Awbery, 1889-1969: Trade union leader: Labour MP for Bristol West.

Sir Cedric Morris, 1889-1982: Noted artist.

Norman Tucker, 1894-1971: Historian, novelist and poet.

Rowe Harding, 1901-1991: Judge, Welsh rugby international and British Lion.

Sir Leslie Joseph, 1908-1992: Leisure industry magnate and philanthropist: son of David Joseph (qv).

Wynford Vaughan-Thomas, 1908-1987: Journalist, author and broadcaster.

Alfred James, 1911-1999: Noted artist.

Dylan Thomas, 1914-1953: Famed poet.

Gilbert Bennett, born 1918: Radio sports commentator.

Harri Webb, 1920-1994: Nationalist, republican, editor and popular poet.

Alun Williams, 1920-1992: Popular broadcaster.

Sir Harry Secombe, 1921-2001: Comedian and singer.

Gil Pendry, 1922-1966: Leading international bowls player.

Trevor Ford, born 1923: Welsh football international.

Gilbert Parkhouse, 1925-2000: Glamorgan and England cricketer.

Sir Melvyn Rosser, 1926-2001: Leading businessman and educationist.

Cliff Curvis, born 1927: Champion welterweight boxer.

Patricia Kern, born 1927: Opera and concert mezzo-soprano.

Ray Daniel, 1928-1997: Welsh football international.

Ivor Allchurch, 1929-1007: Welsh football international: Welsh Sports Personality of the Year 1962.

Paul Ferris, born 1929: Journalist and author.

David Goldstone, born 1929: Lawyer and property company executive.

John Morgan, 1929-1988:
Journalist, broadcaster and
author.

Peter Owen Price, born 1930:
Senior naval chaplain:
chaplain to the Queen 1981-
1984.

James Cellan-Jones, born 1931:
Film and television producer.

John Charles, born 1931:
Outstanding Welsh football
international.

Terry Medwin, born 1932:
Welsh football international.

Len Allchurch, born 1933:
Welsh football international,
brother of Ivor (qv).

Michael Heseltine, born 1933:
Leading Conservative
politician.

Stuart Evans, 1934-1994: Poet
and novelist.

Mel Charles, born 1935: Welsh
international footballer,
brother of John.

Bryn Griffiths, born 1935: Poet.

Cliff Jones, born 1935: Welsh
football international.

Mary Thomas, 1935-1997: Opera
and concert mezzo-soprano.

Mike Davies, born 1936: Leading
tennis player: British hard-
court champion 1960.

Brian Curvis, born 1937:
Champion welterweight
boxer, brother of Cliff:
Welsh Sports Personality of
the Year 1960.

Mel Nurse, born 1937: Welsh
football international.

Cynog Dafis, born 1938: Plaid
Cymru AM for Ceredigion.

Tony Lewis, born 1938:
Glamorgan and England
cricketer, broadcaster and
Chairman of Wales Tourist
Board: Welsh Sports
Personality of the Year 1969.

Donald Anderson, born 1939:
Labour MP for Swansea East.

Iris Gower, born 1939:
Popular novelist.

Garel Rhys, born 1940:
Economist Cardiff Business
School, authority on
automobile industry.

Barry Hole, born 1942: Welsh
football international.

Desmond Barrit, born 1944:
Author and actor.

Martyn Lewis, born 1945:
Television newscaster and
author.

Gary Sprake, born 1945:
Welsh football international.

Mervyn Davies, born 1946:
Welsh rugby international,
British Lion 1971 and 1974:
Welsh Sports Personality of
the year 1976.

Eiddwen Harry, born 1949:
Opera and concert singer.

Roger Blyth, born 1950: Welsh
rugby international.

Geoff Wheel, born 1951:
Welsh rugby international.

Mark Thomas, born 1956:
Composer of film and
television music.

Jeremy Charles, born 1959:
Welsh football international,
son of Mel Charles (qv).

Mark Titley, born 1959: Welsh
rugby international.

Malcolm Dacey, born 1960: Welsh rugby international.

Tracy Edwards, born 1962: Round-the-world yachts-woman.

Peter Harris, born 1962: Champion featherweight boxer.

Huw Warren, born 1963: Jazz musician, composer and arranger.

Dean Saunders, born 1964: Welsh football international.

Phillip Cottey, born 1966: Glamorgan cricketer.

Tony Clement, born 1967: Welsh rugby international, British Lion 1989.

Richard Webster, born 1967: Welsh rugby international.

Robert Croft, born 1970: Glamorgan and England cricketer.

Christian Bale, born 1974: Hollywood film actor.

SYCARTH (Denbighshire)

Owain Glyndŵr (Owain ap Gruffydd ap Madog), c.1349-c.1416: Soldier, leader of last attempt to regain Welsh independence: crowned Prince of Wales 1404.

T

TAFFS WELL (Rhondda Cynon Taff)

Gwyn Williams, born 1918: Welsh rugby league international.

Bleddyn Williams, born 1923: Welsh rugby international British Lion 1950: brother of Gwyn.

Lloyd Williams, born 1933: Welsh rugby international: brother of Bleddyn and Gwyn.

Chris Monger, born 1950: Film director and writer.

TAIBACH (Neath – Port Talbot)

Philip Jones, 1855-1945: Renowned Calvinistic Methodist preacher.

Bill Beynon, 1890-1932: Champion bantamweight boxer.

Sir Anthony Hopkins, born 1937: Leading stage and screen actor: winner of Hollywood Oscar for Best Actor 1996.

TALACRE (Flintshire)

Francis Mostyn, 1860-1939: Catholic Archbishop of Cardiff 1920-1939.

TALGARTH (Powys)

Geoff Lewis, born 1935: leading jockey and trainer: only Welshman to have ridden a Derby winner, 1971.

TALLEY (Powys)
Sir William Davies, 1901-1931:
Journalist, editor of the
'Western Mail' from 1901.

TALSARNAU (Gwynedd)
Anne Harriet Hughes (Gwyneth
Vaughan), 1852-1910: Novelist
and temperance campaigner.
Sir Alfred Charles Glyn Egerton,
1886-1959: Distinguished
chemist.

TALYBONT (Cardiganshire)
John James Williams (J.J.),
1869-1954: Poet and short
story writer: winner of the
National Eisteddfod Chair
1906 and 1908: Archdruid
of Wales 1936-1939.
Thomas Richards, 1878-1962:
Historian.
John Morris, born 1931: Barrister
and senior Labour politician:
MP for Aberavon.

TALYBONT (Gwynedd)
Geraint Gruffydd, born 1928:
Scholar and critic: former
Director of University of
Wales Centre for Advanced
Celtic Studies, Aberystwyth.

TALYBONT-ON-USK (Powys)
Roland Mathias, born 1915:
Poet and literary critic.

TAL-Y-SARN (Gwynedd)
Owain Llewelyn Owain, 1878-
1956: Journalist and author.
Robert Williams Parry, 1884-
1956: Poet, winner of National
Eisteddfod Chair 1910.
Gwilym R. Jones, 1903-1933:
Award-winning poet.

John Selwyn Lloyd, born
1931: Children's writer.

TANYCASTELL (Gwynedd)
John Jones (Talsarn), 1796-
1857: Prominent Calvinistic
Methodist preacher.

TANYGRISIAU (Gwynedd)
Gwyn Thomas, born 1936:
Award-winning poet and
Welsh language scholar.

TENBY (Pembrokeshire)
Robert Recorde, died 1558:
Mathematician who
devised the equals (=) sign.
Arthur Leonard Leach, 1869-
1957: Historian and
geographer.
Augustus John, 1878-1961:
Renowned painter.
Dick Francis, born 1920:
Leading crime writer.
Kenneth Griffith, born 1921:
Actor and writer.
Samantha Wyne Rhydderch,
born 1967: Poet.

TINTERN (Monmouthshire)
John Callice, fl.1560s-1570s:
Cardiff-based pirate.

**TIR-Y-BERTH (Rhondda
Cynon Taff)**
Doug Mountjoy, born 1942:
Leading snooker player:
world amateur champion
1976.

TONDU (Bridgend)
Brinley Roderick Rees, born
1919: Greek scholar.

TONGWYNLAIS (Cardiff)

Dennis 'Hurricane' David, 1918-2000: World War Two fighter ace.

Ian Stephens, born 1952: Welsh rugby international, British Lion 1980 and 1983.

TON PENTRE (Rhondda Cynon Taff)

John Morgan Lloyd, 1880-1960: Professor of Music, University College Cardiff.

Gareth Alban Davies, born 1926: Poet and scholar.

Owain Arwel Hughes, born 1942: Leading orchestral conductor: son of Arwel Hughes (qv).

TONTEG (Rhondda Cynon Taff)

Hopkin Morgan, 1856-1931: Founder of leading south Wales bakery business.

Kelly Morgan, born 1975: Leading badminton player; Commonwealth Games gold medallist 1998.

TONYPANDY (Rhondda Cynon Taff)

Richard (Dick) Lewis, 1877-1953: Veteran Rhondda showman and theatre and cinema manager.

Willie Llewellyn, 1878-1973: Welsh rugby international, British Lion 1904.

Emrys Hughes, 1894-1969: Labour MP for South Ayrshire 1946-1969.

Donald Houston, 1923-1991: Leading actor.

Glyn Houston, born 1926: Leading actor and brother of Donald.

Gwynne Edwards, born 1937: Authority on the theatre in Spain.

David (Dai) Smith, born 1945: Historian and Head of BBC Radio Wales.

Mike Griffiths, born 1962: Welsh rugby international and British Lion 1987.

TONYREFAIL (Rhondda Cynon Taff)

Albert Charles Willis, 1876-1954: President, Australian Labour Party 1923-1925.

Bryn Davies, born 1932: Leading trade unionist.

TOWYN (Conwy)

Robert Davies Owen, 1989-1956: Leading ear and throat specialist.

TRAETH GOCH (Anglesey)

Ifor Owen Thomas, 1892-1956: Popular operatic tenor: photographer and artist.

Einir John, born 1950: Poet.

TRALLWNG (Powys)

Philip Powell, 1594-1646: Catholic priest hanged, drawn and quartered at Tyburn for treason.

Thomas Jeffrey Llewellyn Prichard, 1796-1875: Writer of popular Twm Siôn Catti stories.

TRAWSFYNYDD (Gwynedd)

John Roberts, 1576-1610: Benedictine monk executed at Tyburn for treason.

Huw Ellis, 1714-1774: Skilled player of the Welsh triple harp.

Maurice Jones, 1863-1957: Theologian: Principal of St David's College, Lampeter 1923-1938.

Elis Humphrey Evans (Hedd Wyn), 1887-1917: Poet, posthumous winner of the National Eisteddfod Chair 1917 after his death in action in France.

Robert John (Prysor) Williams, 1891-1967: Actor.

John Rowlands, born 1938: Award-winning novelist.

TREALAW (Rhondda Cynon Taff)

John Warner, 1911-1980: Welsh football international.

Donald Ward, born 1934: Glamorgan cricketer.

Ray Smith, 1936-1991: Leading actor.

TREBANOG (Rhondda Cynon Taff)

Cliff Morgan, born 1930: Welsh rugby international, British Lion 1950: one-time Head of BBC Outside Broadcasts.

TREBANOS (Swansea)

Ogwyn Davies, born 1925: Artist.

Greg Thomas, born 1960: Glamorgan and England cricketer.

Bleddyn Bowen, born 1961: Welsh rugby international.

Robert Jones, born 1965: Welsh rugby international, British Lion 1987.

TRECASTLE (Powys)

David Jenkins, 1848-1915: Noted composer, editor and educationist.

TRECYNON (Rhondda Cynon Taff)

Griffith Rhys Jones (Caradog), 1834-1897: Conductor of the acclaimed 'Côr Mawr', winners at the Crystal Palace Festival in 1872 and 1873.

Dewi Watkin Powell, born 1920: Judge and public servant.

TREDEGAR (Blaenau Gwent)

Moses Russell, 1888-1946: Welsh football international.

Aneurin Bevan, 1897-1960: Senior Labour MP, responsible for the introduction of the National Health Service.

Sir Archibald (Archie) Lush, 1900-1976: Schools inspector: Chair Welsh Hospitals Board.

Diana Lodge, 1906-1998: Noted painter.

Philip Weekes, born 1920: Area Director of National Coal Board 1973-1985: public servant.

Ray Reardon, born 1932: Six times world professional snooker champion.

Cliff Wilson, 1934-1994: World amateur snooker champion 1978.

Dame Margaret Price, born 1941: Leading operatic soprano.

Neil Kinnock, born 1942: Labour Party leader 1983-1992: Vice President European Commission.

Robat Powel, born 1948: Poet, in 1985 the first person who had learned Welsh to win a National Eisteddfod Chair.

Berwyn Price, born 1951: Leading track athlete: Welsh Sports Personality of the Year 1973.

Christopher Meredith, born 1954: Award-winning poet and novelist.

Steve Jones, born 1955: Marathon runner: in 1988 the first Briton to win the New York Marathon: Welsh Sports Personality of the Year 1985.

Wayne Jones, born 1959: Leading snooker player.

TREFDRAETH (Anglesey)

Rowland Williams (Hwfa Môn), 1825-1905: Poet, winner of the National Eisteddfod Crown 1867: Archdruid of Wales 1895-1905.

TREFECA (Powys)

Howell Harris, 1714-1773: Leader of the 1735 Methodist Revival – 'the Great Awakening'.

TREFIL (Blaenau Gwent)

Denzil Williams, born 1938: Welsh rugby international, British Lion 1966.

TRE-FIN (Pembrokeshire)

Edgar Phillips (Trefin), 1889-1962: Winner of National Eisteddfod Chair 1933: Archdruid of Wales 1960-1962.

TREFOR (Anglesey)

Sir John Morris-Jones, 1864-1929: Welsh language scholar and poet.

Alun Jones, born 1946: Award-winning novelist.

TREFOREST (Rhondda Cynon Taff)

Daniel Radcliffe, 1860-1933: Cardiff shipowner.

Morfydd Llwyn Owen, 1891-1918: Composer and pianist.

Meic Stephens, born 1938: Journalist, author and editor: founder of 'Poetry Wales'.

Tom Jones (Thomas Jones Woodward), born 1940: International singing star.

TREFRIW (Gwynedd)

David Jones, 1708-1785: One of the first Welsh printers.

Evan Evans (Ieuan Glan Geirionydd), 1795-1855: Anglican clergyman, poet and editor.

TREFEGLWYS (Powys)

Richard Thomas, 1890-1977: Principal, Bangor Normal College.

TREGARON (Cardiganshire)

Thomas Jones (Twm Sion Catti), c.1530-1609: Leading landowner and noted prankster about whom numerous fiction accounts have been written.

Henry Richard, 1812-1888: Prominent Liberal politician known as 'the Member for Wales'.

William Evans, 1896-1988:
Leading cardiologist.
Sir John Rowland, 1897-1940:
Chairman, Welsh Board of
Health.
Marged Pritchard, born 1919:
Prize-winning novelist.

TREGARTH (Gwynedd)
Sir Ifor Williams, 1881-1965:
Welsh language scholar.

TREGYNON (Powys)
Morgan Jones, 1839-1926: Major
railway builder in Texas.

TREHARRIS (Merthyr Tydfil)
John Griffiths, 1907-1980:
Children's writer.
Ifor Davies, born 1938:
Painter and lecturer.

TREHERBERT (Rhondda Cynon Taff)
W. G. Cove, 1888-1963:
Labour MP for Aberavon.
Gareth Howel Williams, born
1925: Leading chemist.
Charles Burton, born 1929:
Noted painter.
Tudor Bowen, 1934-1994:
Pioneer of Welsh Studies
courses, Trinity College,
Carmarthen.
T. Arfon Williams, 1935-1998:
Poet specialising in
englynion (strict metre).

TRELLECK (Monmouthshire)
Bertrand Russell (Earl), 1872-
1970: Renowned philosopher
and writer.

TREMADOG (Gwynedd)
Thomas Edward (T.E.)
Lawrence (Lawrence of
Arabia), 1888-1935: Scholar,
soldier and writer.
Michael Povey, born 1950:
Playwright and actor.
Eric Jones, born 1937: Crew
member of first hot air
balloon to fly over Mount
Everest, 1991.

TREORCHY (Rhondda Cynon Taff)
Euros Bowen, 1904-1988: Poet,
winner of the National
Eisteddfod Crown 1948
and 1950.
W.J. (Billy) Cleaver, born 1921:
Welsh rugby international.
Margaret Pomeroy, born 1922:
Leading bowls player.
Ceri Lewis, born 1926: Welsh
language scholar and
historian.
Rhoslyn Davies, 1929-1962:
Orchestral conductor.
Clive Thomas, born 1936:
Leading football referee: in
1976 the third Welshman to
referee a Wembley FA Cup
Final.
Geraint Cynan, born 1961:
Folk musician, member of
'Bwchadanas'.

TRE'R DDOL (Cardiganshire)
Humphrey Rowland Jones,
1832-1895: Leader of the
major 1855 religious revival.
Dic Jones, born 1934: Poet,
winner of the Chair at the
Urdd Eisteddfod five times
and at the National
Eisteddfod 1966.

TRE'R DDOL (Denbighshire)
Thomas Jones, 1648-1713:
Publisher of first Welsh
almanacks and compiler of
a Welsh-English dictionary
1688.

TREVINE (Pembrokeshire)
Francis Jones, 1908-1993: Herald
Extraordinary in Wales.

TREWALCHMAI (Anglesey)
Gwalchmai ap Meilyr, fl. 1130-
1180: Court poet to Owain
ap Gruffydd, ruler of
Gwynedd.

TRIMSARAN
(Carmarthenshire)
Les Williams, born 1922:
Welsh rugby international
in both codes.
Jonathan Davies, born 1962:
Welsh rugby international
in both codes and television
sports broadcaster.

TROEDYRHIW (Merthyr Tydfil)
Enoch Morrell, 1860-1934:
Miners' leader; first Labour
mayor in Wales at Merthyr
Tydfil 1905-1906.
Richard Livsey (Lord), born
1935: Liberal Democrat
party leader in Wales.
Alun Francis, born 1943:
Orchestral conductor.

TUMBLE (Carmarthenshire)
Leslie Jones, born 1917:
Economist and public servant.

TYCROES (Carmarthenshire)
Alan Watkins, born 1933:
Leading London journalist.

TYLORSTOWN (Rhondda Cynon Taff)
Mansel Thomas, 1909-1986:
Composer and conductor.
Gwilym Davies (Lord), 1913-
1992: Labour politician.
Gareth Hywel Jones, born 1930:
Authority on English law.
John Bevan, born 1950: Welsh
rugby international, 'British
Lion' 1971.

TYNANT (Denbighshire)
John Williams (ab Ithel), 1811-
1862: Antiquary and author:
founder member of the
Cambrian Archaeological
Association 1847.

TYWYN (Gwynedd)
Griffith Evans, 1835-1935:
Leading bacteriologist.
Robert Pugh Rowlands, 1874-
1933: Leading surgeon.
Edward Ernest Hughes, 1877-
1953: First Professor of
History at University
College, Swansea and
broadcaster.
Thomas Richards, 1909-1998:
Playwright and journalist.
Gwilym Prys-Davies (Lord),
born 1923: Lawyer and
public servant.

U

USK (Monmouthshire)
Adam of Usk, 1352?-1430:
Chronicler: supporter of
Owain Glyndŵr (qv).
Phil Clift, born 1918:
Glamorgan cricketer.

Allan Watkins, born 1922:
Glamorgan and England
cricketer.
Paul Murphy, born 1948: Labour
MP for Torfaen: Secretary of
State for Wales 1999.

V

VARTEG (Blaenau Gwent)
Arthur Jenkins, died 1946:
Miners' leader and Labour
MP: father of Roy Jenkins
(qv).

VAYNOR (Powys)
Trevor Stanley Jones, 1867-
1939: Coalowner and
Cardiff shipowner.

VELFREY (Pembrokeshire)
Glyn Daniel, 1914-1986:
Archaeologist, writer and
broadcaster.

VELINDRE
(Carmarthenshire)
Alan Jones, born 1938:
Glamorgan cricketer.
Eifion Jones, born 1942:
Glamorgan cricketer,
brother of Alan.

W

WATFORD (Caerphilly)
David Williams, 1738-1816:
Radical political thinker.

WATTSVILLE (Caerphilly)
Clive Westlake, born 1936:
Composer of popular
songs.

WAUNFAWR (Gwynedd)
John Evans, 1770-1799:
Explorer who mapped
some 2,000 miles of the
Mississippi River.
Sir Henry Morris-Jones, 1884-
1972: Liberal MP and
public servant.
Hywel David Lewis, 1910-1992:
Historian and philosopher.

WELSHPOOL (Powys)

Richard Davies, 1635-1708: Leading Quaker.

Sarah Winifred Parry (Winnie Parry), 1870-1953: Author and editor.

William Waring, 1885-1918: Awarded the Victoria Cross posthumously in France.

Emyr Estyn Evans, 1905-1989: Distinguished geographer.

John Gittins, born 1951: Member of 'Plethyn' folk group.

Roy Griffiths, born 1952: Member of 'Plethyn' folk group.

Patrick Thomas, born 1952: Clergyman and writer: member of the Welsh Language Board.

Linda Healy, born 1958: Member of 'Plethyn' folk group.

WENVOE (Vale of Glamorgan)

Frederick Jennings Thomas, 1786-1855: Rear-admiral, participated in the Battle of Trafalgar.

WHITCHURCH (Cardiff)

Will Paynter, 1903-1984: Miners' leader: President of the National Union of Miners 1957-1968.

WHITCHURCH-IN-CEMAIS (Pembrokeshire)

Daniel Rees, 1855-1931: Journalist and editor.

WHITFORD (Flintshire)

Thomas Pennant, 1726-1798: Naturalist and author.

WHITLAND (Pembrokeshire)

William Mathias, 1934-1992: Distinguished composer.

WREXHAM

William Davis, 1627-1690: Highwayman, hanged in London.

George Jeffreys, 1645-1690: Lord Chancellor of England 1685-1688: notorious as 'the hanging judge'.

Sir William Lloyd, 1782-1857: Soldier and early European Himalayan climber.

Charles James Apperley (Nimrod), 1779-1843: Noted sports writer.

John Powell, 1860-1947: Welsh international footballer.

Sir Arthur Griffith-Boscawen, 1865-1946: Conservative MP and public servant.

Ted Robbins, 1868-1946: Secretary of Football Association of Wales.

Hugh Hamshaw Thomas, 1885-1962: Leading palaeontologist.

A. H. Dodd, 1891-1975: Distinguished historian.

J. G. Parry Thomas, 1894-1927: Racing driver, holder of world land speed records: killed at Pendine.

Fulke Walwyn, 1910-1991: Grand National winning jockey 1936.

Islwyn Ffowc Elis, born 1924: Novelist.

Bedwyr Lewis Jones, 1933-1992: Critic and scholar.

Martin Thomas, born 1937:
Lawyer and Liberal
Democrat politician.

John Williams, born 1937:
Leading snooker player.

Arfon Griffiths, born 1941:
Welsh football international;
Welsh Sports Personality of
the Year 1975.

Philip Owens, born 1947:
Award-winning poet.

Anne Williams-King, born
1961: Leading operatic
soprano.

WYNDHAM (Bridgend)
James Davies, 1886-1917:
Awarded the Victoria Cross
posthumously in France.

Y

YNYSDDU (Torfaen)
William Thomas (Islwyn):
1832-1978: Noted poet and
Calvinist minister.

Trevor Thomas, 1907-1993:
Leading art historian.

**YNYSHIR (Rhondda Cynon
Taff)**
Dan Jones, 1908-1985: Trade
union official and Labour
MP for Burnley.

**YNYSYBWL (Rhondda
Cynon Taff)**
Leonard Hall (Viscount),
1913-1985: Surgeon and
businessman.

Ken Rowlands, born 1936:
International rugby referee.

Leighton Rees, born 1940: First
world darts champion 1977.

Garin Jenkins, born 1967:
Welsh rugby international.

**YSBYTY IFAN
(Denbighshire)**
Elis Prys (Price), 1512-1594:
'The Red Doctor', visitor
for the dissolution of the
monasteries.

William Cynwal, died 1587:
Notable poet.

**YSTALYFERA
(Carmarthenshire)**
David Vaughan Thomas,
1873-1934: Composer.

Islwyn Williams, 1903-1957:
Short story writer.

Wynne Samuel, 1912-1989:
Barrister and Plaid Cymru
activist.

John Ellis Caerwyn Williams,
1912-1999: Celtic scholar
and educationist.

Aneurin Thomas, born 1921:
Director Welsh Arts
Council 1967-1984.

Thomas Arfon Owen, born
1933: Director Welsh Arts
Council from 1984.

YSTRADFELLTE (Powys)

John Hartman Morgan, 1876-
1955: Distinguished
constitutional lawyer and
academic.

YSTRAD FFLUR (see Strata Florida)

YSTRADGYNLAIS (Powys)

Thomas Levi, 1825-1916:
Author and hymnwriter:
'king of the Methodists of
Carmarthenshire'.

Sir Tudur Thomas, 1893-1976:
Leading ophthalmic surgeon.

Stephen Joseph Williams,
1896-1992: Welsh language
scholar.

Sir Goronwy Hopkin Daniel,
born 1914: Senior civil
servant and educationist.

Menna Gallie, 1920-1990:
Novelist.

Ewart Alexander, born 1931:
Novelist and playwright.

YSTRAD MEURIG (Cardiganshire)

John Williams, 1792-1858:
Educationist: first rector of
the Edinburgh Academy
and first Warden of
Llandovery College.

YSTRAD MYNACH (Caerphilly)

Janet Ackland, born 1938:
Leading bowls player:
world women's singles
outdoor champion 1988.

Andy Fairweather Low, born
1949: Founder of the
successful 'Amen Corner'
band of the 1960s.

YSTRAD RHONDDA (Rhondda Cynon Taff)

Sir Ben Bowen Thomas, 1899-
1977: Leading educationist:
Warden College Harlech
1927-1940: Senior member
of UNESCO, Paris, 1954-1960.

Rex Willis, 1924-2000: Welsh
rugby international, British
Lion 1950.

Ernest Zobole, 1927-1999:
Leading painter.

Mel Hopkins, born 1934:
Welsh football international.

REST OF THE BRITISH ISLES

ENGLAND

APPLEDORE (Devon)

Sir William Reardon Smith, 1856-1935: Leading Cardiff shipowner and philanthropist.

James Tatem (Lord Glanely), 1868-1942: Leading Cardiff shipowner and public servant.

BACTON (Hereford and Worcester)

Blanche Parry, 1508?-1590: Nurse and favoured attendant to Elizabeth I.

BIDEFORD (Devon)

John Cory, 1828-1910: Coalowner and Cardiff shipowner.

BIRKENHEAD (Cheshire)

David Thomas Gruffydd Evans (Lord Evans of Claughton), 1928-1992: Liberal politician and public servant.

Marion Eames, born 1921: Novelist.

BIRMINGHAM

Sir Edward Burne-Jones, 1833-1898: Distinguished artist.

Sir Charles Wright, 1876-1950: Leading South Wales iron and steel magnate.

Gwilym Lewis, 1897-1996: First World War fighter ace.

William Condry, 1918-1998: Naturalist and author.

Alexander Numa Labinsky (Count), 1925-1994: Compac disc (CD) pioneer: founder of Nimbus Records, Monmouth.

Sheenagh Pugh, born 1950: Award-winning poet.

Rupert Moon, born 1968: Welsh rugby international.

BODMIN (Cornwall)

Henry Dennis, 1825-1906: Successful exploiter of north-east Wales coal and lead resources.

BRENTWOOD (Essex)

Hanning Phillips, 1904-1998: Businessman: donor of Picton Castle for Graham Sutherland Gallery 1976.

BRIGHTON (East Sussex)

Gerald Morgan, born 1936: Author and editor.

BRISTOL

Jean Earle, born 1909: Award-winning poet.

Peter Walker, born 1936: Glamorgan and England cricketer.

BURNOPFIELD (County Durham)

Jim McConnon, born 1922: Glamorgan and England cricketer.

BROCKLEY (Kent)

David Jones, 1895-1971: Artist and writer.

CHEADLE (Cheshire)

Mathew Prichard, born 1943: Chair of Welsh Arts Council 1986.

CHESTER (Cheshire)

John Owen (Owain Alaw), 1821-1883: Collector and composer: his 'Prince of Wales' said to be the first Welsh secular cantata.

Sir Edward Anwyl, 1866-1914: Celtic scholar, educationist and public servant.

John Bodvan Anwyl, 1875-1949: Author, editor and compiler of an English-Welsh dictionary: brother of Sir Edward.

CHICHESTER (West Sussex)

Sir Eric Ommaney Skaife, 1884-1956: Brigadier, supporter of Welsh cultural organisations like the Cymmrodorion Society and the Urdd.

CHIPPENHAM (Wiltshire)

Sir Cyril Fox, 1882-1967: Archaeologist: Director of the National Museum of Wales.

CHIPPING NORTON (Oxfordshire)

Harry Packer, 1868-1946: Welsh rugby international and senior rugby administrator.

Walter Padley, 1916-1984: Labour MP for Ogmore.

CHIPPING SODBURY (Gloucestershire)

William Watts, 1870-1950: Welsh rugby international.

CLEVEDON (Somerset)

Jan Morris, born 1926: Leading journalist and author.

CLIFFORD (Hereford and Worcester)

John Miles, 1621-1683: Baptist leader: founder of Swanzey, Massachusetts.

CLIFTON (Cumbria)

John Wilkinson, 1728-1808: North Wales ironmaster at Bersham and Brymbo.

CORBY (Northamptonshire)

Gareth Price, born 1939: Senior BBC administrator.

DUDLEY (Hereford and Worcester)

Harri Pritchard Jones, born 1933: Award-winning novelist and short story writer.

DURHAM (County Durham)

Jonah Jones, born 1919: Distinguished artist.

EASTWOOD (Nottinghamshire)
Richard Donner, 1871-1951:
  Pioneer cinema chain
  owner in South Wales.

EPWORTH (Lincolnshire)
Sir Idris Bell, 1879-1967:
  Eminent literary critic.

EXETER (Devon)
Peter Lord, born 1948:
  Sculptor and art historian.

FARNHAM (Surrey)
Iwan Thomas, born 1974:
  Olympic silver medallist,
  track relay 1996; Welsh
  Sports Personality of the
  Year 1998.

FARNWORTH (Lancashire)
Alfred Mond, 1868-1930:
  Founder of Mond Nickel
  Works, Clydach, first Chair
  of ICI: Liberal MP.

GATESHEAD (County Durham)
Ossie Wheatley, born 1935:
  Glamorgan cricketer, England
  Test selector and Chair of
  Welsh Sports Council.

GAYTON (Northamptonshire)
Sir Clough Williams-Ellis,
  1883-1978: Architect and
  town planner: creator of
  Portmeirion holiday village.

GOBOWEN (Shropshire)
Arthur Boucher, 1870-1948:
  Welsh rugby international.

HALIFAX (West Yorkshire)
Arnold Dyson, 1905-1978:
  Glamorgan cricketer.

HARDENHUISH (Hereford and Worcester)
Francis Kilvert, 1840-1879:
  Cleric and diarist.

HEREFORD (Hereford and Worcester)
John Davies, 1565?-1618:
  Noted poet.
Trevor Fishlock, born 1941:
  Journalist, broadcaster and
  author.

ILLOGAN (Cornwall)
Richard Trevithick, 1771-1833:
  Engineer responsible for
  the world's first steam
  locomotive which ran from
  Penydarren to Abercynon
  in 1804.

KNOTTINGLEY (West Yorkshire)
William Lascelles Carr, 1841-
  1902: Editor-in-Chief and
  proprietor of the 'Western
  Mail'.

KENDAL (Cumbria)
Richard Fothergill, 1758-1821:
  Sirhowy ironmaster.

LACOCK (Wiltshire)
Cyril Smart, 1898-1975:
  Glamorgan cricketer.

LEEDS (West Yorkshire)
John Aloysius Ward, born
  1929: Archbishop of Cardiff.

LEICESTER

James Harvey Insole, 1821-1901: Leading Cardiff shipowner.

Douglas Clark Stephen, 1894-1960: Editor 'South Wales Echo'.

LITTLE LEVER (Lancashire)

Ned Thomas, born 1936: Author and editor: founder of 'Planet' magazine 1970.

LIVERPOOL

Felicia Dorothea Hemans, 1793-1835: Poet.

Sir John Lloyd, 1861-1947: Distinguished historian.

Lady Ruth Ellis, 1871-1946: Collector of Welsh folk music.

Thomas Alwyn Lloyd, 1881-1960: Architect, town planner and public servant.

Alfred Francis, 1901-1985: Executive Chair Welsh National Opera 1968-1975, Vice Chair TWW (commercial televison) 1959-1968.

James Hanley, 1901-1985: Award-winning novelist.

Thomas Jones Pierce, 1905-1964: Noted historian.

John Roberts, 1906-1965: Welsh rugby international.

Dewi-Prys Thomas, 1916-1985: First Professor of Architecture, University of Wales 1964-1981.

Stuart Lloyd Jones, 1917-1998: Chief Executive/Town Clerk of Cardiff 1970-1974: supervised 1979 referendum count.

Sir Hywel Wyn Evans, 1920-1988: Educationist and public servant.

Gwenith Lilly, born 1920: Children's writer.

Emrys Roberts (Emrys Deudraeth) born 1929: Poet, winner of National Eisteddfod Chair 1967 and 1971; Archdruid of Wales 1987-1990.

Alice Thomas Ellis, born 1932: Award-winning novelist.

LONDON

John Dee, 1527-1608: Mathematician, astronomer, alchemist.

Katherine Phillips (The Matchless Orina), 1631-1664: Minor poet who married into a leading Welsh family.

Anthony Bacon, 1718-1786: Pioneer ironmaster at Hirwaun and Merthyr Tydfil.

David Thompson (ap Thomas), 1770-1837: Explorer in British North America, first European to descend the Colombia River 1811: Thompson River, British Colombia named after him.

Owen Jones, 1809-1874: Architect: supervisor of works for 1851 Great Exhibition.

John Orlando Parry, 1810-1879: Successful composer and singer: son of John Parry (Bardd Alaw) (qv).

Father Ignatius (Joseph Leycester Lyne), 1837-1908: Monk who founded Llanthony Abbey, Monmouthshire 1870.

Sidney Gilchrist Thomas, 1850-1885: Innovative metallurgist.

Mary Davies, 1855-1933: Celebrated soprano: Welsh folk song enthusiast.

Ernest Rhys, 1859-1946: Poet, author and editor.

Owen Glynne Jones, 1867-1899: Mountaineer and founder member of the Climbers Club 1898.

Edward Thomas, 1878-1917: Noted poet.

Thomas Iorwerth Ellis, 1879-1970: Author and educationist.

Sir William Herbert Poyer Lewis, 1881-1950: Judge and public servant.

Sir David James, 1887-1967: London cinema owner, businessman and philanthopist.

Dame Gwen Ffrangcon-Davies, 1889-1992: Leading actress.

Leonard David Williams, 1894-1950: Managing Director Ocean-National Collieries before nationalisation.

Jenkin Alban Davies, 1901-1968: Businessman and philanthropist: Welsh language supporter.

Sir Julian Hodge, born 1904: Cardiff-based banker and financier.

George Chapman, 1908-1993: Noted artist.

A. H. A. Hogg, 1908-1989: Secretary, Royal Society for Ancient Monuments in Wales.

Iorwerth Eiddon Stephen Edwards, 1909-1996: Leading Egyptologist.

Margiad Evans, 1909-1958: Children's author.

Arthur Giardelli, born 1911: Artist.

Dafydd Jenkins, born 1911: Critic and historian.

Harri Gwyn, 1913-1985: Author and journalist.

Les Muncer, 1913-1982: Glamorgan cricketer.

C. W. L. (Bill) Bevan, 1920-1989: Controversial Principal of University College Cardiff.

David Tinker, born 1924: Noted artist.

Raymond Garlick, born 1926: Poet and editor.

Windsor Davies, born 1930: Popular actor.

David Gwilym Lloyd Evans, 1933-1990: Glamorgan cricketer and Test umpire.

Kenneth O. Morgan, born 1934: Leading historian: award-winning writer.

Sally Roberts Jones, born 1935: Award-winning poet.

John Merriman, 1936-1999: Commonwealth Games silver medallist, six miles, 1958.

John Taylor, born 1943: Welsh rugby international, British Lion 1968 and 1971: sports broadcaster.

David Tress, born 1955: Painter.

Glyn Hodges, born 1963:
Welsh football international.

Joe Calzaghe, born 1972:
Champion super-
middleweight boxer.

LUDLOW (Shropshire)

Thomas Johnes, 1748-1816:
Landscape enthusiast in
Cardiganshire.

LYDNEY (Gloucestershire)

Stephen James, born 1966:
Glamorgan cricketer.

MACCLESFIELD (Cheshire)

Charles Tunnicliffe, 1901-
1979: Noted artist.

MADLEY (Hereford and Worcester)

Bert Coombes, 1894-1974:
Autobiographical writer
and miner.

MANCHESTER

John Roberts, 1823-1893:
Billiards champion of
England 1849-1870.

David Lloyd George (Earl of
Dwyfor), 1863-1945: Prime
Minister 1916-1922: Liberal
Party Leader.

R. T. Jenkins, 1881-1964:
Leading historian.

Sir John Goronwy Edwards,
1891-1976: Distinguished
historian.

William Evans Hoyle, died
1920: First Director
National Museum of Wales
1909-1924.

Richard Lewis, 1914-1990:
Leading opera and concert
tenor.

Carl Clowes, born 1943:
Physician and business
innovator.

MIDDLESBOROUGH (Cleveland)

Iolo Aneurin Williams, 1890-
1962: Author, journalist and
public servant.

NORMANTON (West Yorkshire)

Richard Crawshay, 1739-1810:
Cyfarthfa ironmaster:
leading promoter of the
Glamorganshire Canal.

NORTHAM (Devon)

Sir George Stapledon, 1889-
1960: First head of Welsh
Plant Breeding Station,
Aberystwyth.

NORTHAMPTON

Nigel Wells, born 1944:
Award-winning poet.

NORWICH (Norfolk)

Ruch Madoc, born 1943:
Popular actress.

NOTTINGHAM

Bert Winfield, 1878-1919:
Welsh rugby international.

Jamie Baulch, born 1973:
Olympic silver medallist,
track relay 1996.

OLDHAM (Lancashire)

Matthew Maynard, born 1966: Glamorgan and England cricketer.

OSWESTRY (Shropshire)

Gutun Owain, fl1450-1498: Major late medieval poet and genealogist.

Maurice Kyffin, c.1558-1598: Solider and writer.

Edward Lhuyd, 1660?-1709: Outstanding Celtic scholar: second keeper of the Ashmolean Museum, Oxford.

David Christopher Davies, 1827-1885: Geologist and author.

Sir Walford Davies, 1869-1941: Distinguished composer: Master of the King's Music 1934-1941.

Charles Morris, 1880-1957: Welsh football international.

Wilfred Owen, 1893-1918: Celebrated poet.

Ivor Roberts Jones, 1913-1996: Noted artist.

Ian Woosnam, born 1958: Leading golfer: Welsh Sports Personality of the Year 1987, 1990 and 1991.

PADSTOW (Cornwall)

John Cory, 1823-1891: Leading Cardiff shipowner.

John Cory, 1855-1930: Cardiff shipowner: son of John Cory.

Sir Herbert Cory, 1857-1933: Cardiff shipowner, younger son of John Cory.

PLYMOUTH (Devon)

Stuart Rendel, 1834-1913: Liberal politician.

Iolo Jones, born 1955: Member of 'Ar Log' folk group.

PORTSMOUTH (Hampshire)

James Callaghan (Lord Callaghan of Cardiff), born 1912: Labour MP Cardiff South-east and Penarth; Prime Minister, Chancellor of the Exchequer, Foreign Secretary, Home Secretary.

ROADE (Northamptonshire)

Glenys Kinnock, born 1942: Labour politician and MEP: wife of Neil Kinnock (qv).

ROTHERHAM (South Yorkshire)

Daniel Hannon, 1884-1946: Catholic Bishop of Menevia, Wrexham.

ST ALBANS (Hereforshire)

Paul Price, born 1954: Welsh football international.

ST GEORGE'S (Shropshire)

Alfred Onions, 1858-1921: South Wales miners' leader.

SHEERNESS (Kent)

Kenneth Loveland, 1915-1998: Journalist, editor of 'South Wales Argus' 1951-1970: music critic.

SHEFFIELD (South Yorkshire)

Sir Edward Julian Pode, 1902-

1968: Accountant and industrialist: Chair of the Steel Company of Wales 1962-1967.

SHIRLEY (Derbyshire)
John Cowper Powys, 1872-1963: Novelist.

SHREWSBURY (Shropshire)
Lewis Griffith Evans Pugh, died 1994: Physiologist and mountaineer.

SLEAFORD (Lincolnshire)
Gilli Davies, born 1950: Cookery writer and broadcaster.

SOUTHAMPTON (Hampshire)
Clive Betts, born 1943: Journalist and author: Welsh affairs correspondent 'Western Mail'
Dave Roberts, born 1949: Welsh football international.

SOUTHPORT (Lancashire)
Anne Howells, born 1941: Opera and concert mezzo-soprano.

SOUTH SHIELDS (County Durham)
Sir Percy Thomas, 1883-1969: Distinguished architect: elected President Royal Institute of British Architects 1943.

SOUTHWICK (Sussex)
James Mercer, 1895-1987: Glamorgan cricketer.

STOURBRIDGE (Hereford and Worcester)
Alfred Edwin Morris, 1894-1971: Archbishop of Wales 1957-1967.

STRETTON SUGWAS (Hereford and Worcester)
Roger Cadwaladr, 1566-1610: Jesuit seminary priest hanged, drawn and quartered at Leominster for treason.

SURBITON (Surrey)
Sir Alfred Zimmern, 1879-1957: First Professor of International Relations, University College, Aberystwyth.

SUTTON COLDFIELD (Warnickshire)
Colin Charvis, born 1972: Welsh rugby international and British Lion 2001.

TATSFIELD (Surrey)
Owain Lawgoch (Owain ap Thomas ap Rhodri), assassinated 1378: Mercenary captain and claimant to the Principality of Wales. (His birth here is not certain).

TIVERTON (Devon)
Dick Hellings, 1873-1938: Welsh rugby international.

UFFINGTON (Lincolnshire)
Lady Charlotte Guest, 1812-1895: Translator of the 'Mabinogion'.

WAKEFIELD (West Yorkshire)
Crawshay Bailey, 1789-1872:
Nant-y-glo ironmaster:
leading promoter of the
Monmouthshire Canal.

WALLASEY (Cheshire)
Saunders Lewis, 1893-1985:
Major Welsh writer: founder
member of Plaid Cymru.

WEARE (Somerset)
Albert (Billy) Price, 1871-1938:
Welsh rugby international
and administrator.

WEYBRIDGE (Surrey)
Richard Hughes, 1900-1976:
Popular novelist, 'A High
Wind in Jamaica' his best
known book.

**WESTBURY ON SEVERN
(Gloucestershire)**
Gwyn Nicholls, 1874-1939:
Welsh rugby international.

WIVELISCOME (Somerset)
Fred Hancock, 1859-1943:
Welsh rugby international.

WOOKEY (Somerset)
Arthur James Cook, 1884-
1932: Miners' leader during
the 1926 General Strike.

IRELAND

BELFAST

Sir Harry Reichel, 1856-1931:
First Principal of University
College, Bangor.

Eirene White (Baroness), 1909-
1999: Labour politician: in
1964, the first woman MP
from Wales to become a
government minister.

DUBLIN

Gruffydd ap Cynan, died 1137:
Ruler of Gwynedd.

Sarah Ponsonby, 1756?-1831:
One of 'the Ladies of
Llangollen'.

KILKENNY

Eleanor Butler, 1745?-1829:
One of 'the Ladies of
Llangollen'.

Michael Joseph McGrath,
1882-1961: Archbishop of
Cardiff, 1940-1961.

SCOTLAND

AYR
Sir Alex Gordon, 1917-1999:
Leading architect in Wales;
President of the Royal
Institute of British
Architects 1971-73.

CARDROSS
A. J. (Archibald Joseph)
Cronin, 1896-1981: Doctor
and novelist, some of
whose books were set in
the South Wales valleys.

EDINBURGH
David Wilson, born 1935:
Director, Welsh Plant Breeding
Station, Aberystwyth.
Stanley Thomas, born 1941:
Millionaire South Wales
businessman.
Peter Thomas, born 1943:
Millionaire South Wales
businessman, brother of
Stanley.

GIRVAN
Kirsty Wade, born 1961: Track
athlete, Welsh Sports
Personality of the Year 1986
– the first woman to win
this award.

HOLYTOWN
Keir Hardie, 1856-1916:
Pioneer socialist, MP for
Merthyr Tydfil.

LOSSIEMOUTH
James Ramsay MacDonald,
1866-1937: Labour MP for
Aberavon when he became
the first Labour Prime
Minister in 1924.

MOUNT STUART
John Stuart, 2nd Marquis of
Bute, 1793-1848: 'The
creator of Cardiff':
landowner, docks and
railway builder, coalowner.
John Patrick Crichton Stuart, 3rd
Marquis of Bute, 1847-1900:
Landowner, coalowner,
scholar and antiquarian,
philanthropist.

'THE OLD NORTH' (present southern Scotland and northern England)
Aneurin, fl.6th century: Poet,
with Taliesin, one of the
earliest writers in Welsh.
Gildas, fl.6th century: Monk
and author of 'The Ruin of
Britain' criticising
contemporary British
rulers.
Taliesin, fl.6th century: Poet,
with Aneurin, one of the
earliest writers in Welsh.

REST OF EUROPE

BRUGGE/BRUGES (Belgium)
Sir Frank Brangwyn, 1867-
1956: Distinguished artist.

GOTHENBURG (Sweden)
George Osborne Morgan,
1826-1897: Liberal MP.

LENTHE (Germany)
Sir William Siemens, 1823-
1883: Founder of Landore
Steelworks.

MADRID (Spain)
Adelina Patti, 1843-1919:
Internationally famed
operatic diva: settled at
Craig-y-nos Castle,
Swansea Valley.

RHEINDALEN (Germany)
Paul Thorburn, born 1962:
Welsh rugby international
and administrator.

ROTTERDAM (Netherlands)
Roland Lefebre, born 1963:
Glamorgan cricketer: first
Dutchman to score a
century in first class cricket.

WEGBURG (Germany)
Dave Phillips, born 1963:
Welsh football international.

**WITTENBERG-AM-ELBE
(Germany)**
Kate Bosse-Griffiths, 1910-
1998: Egyptologist and
Welsh-language novelist:
wife of John Gwyn Griffiths
(qv), mother of Heini
Gruffudd (qv) and Robat
Gruffudd (qv).

REST OF THE WORLD

ANTIGUA (West Indies)
Viv Richards, born 1952:
   Glamorgan cricketer.

BARBADOS (West Indies)
Tony Cordle, born 1940:
   Glamorgan cricketer.

BOSTON (USA)
Elihu Yale, 1649-1726:
   Merchant co-founder of
   Yale University: High
   Sheriff of Denbighshire.

BOMBAY (India)
Thomas William Pearson,
   1872-1957: Welsh rugby
   and hockey international:
   Welsh doubles tennis
   champion.

BUENOS AIRES (Argentina)
Lynette Roberts, 1909-1995:
   Poet: married Keidrych
   Rhys (qv), friend of Dylan
   Thomas (qv).

CALCUTTA (India)
Sir William Jones, 1746-1794:
   Hindu law scholar.

CAPE TOWN (South Africa)
Llewellyn John Montfort Bell,
   1862-1915: Theologian,
   Principal of St David's
   College, Lampeter.

COLOMBO (Sri Lanka)
Alexander Cordell, 1914-1997:
   Popular author of novels
   set in Wales.

DURBAN (South Africa)
Pat Beavan, born 1951: Welsh
   Commonwealth Games gold
   medallist, swimming 1974.

GRAHAMSTOWN (South Africa)
Win Griffiths, born 1943:
   Labour MP for Bridgend.

JOHANNESBURG (South Africa)
Adrian Dale, born 1968:
   Glamorgan cricketer.
Rodney Ontong, born 1955:
   Glamorgan cricketer.

KITCHENER (Canada)
Charles Alfred Edwards,
   1882-1960: Metallurgist and
   academic: Principal
   University College Swansea.

MELBOURNE (Australia)
Shani Rhys James, born 1953:
   Leading artist.

MOASCAR (Egypt)
Graham Price, born 1951:
   Welsh rugby international
   and British Lion 1977, 1980
   and 1983.

MORRINSVILLE (New Zealand)

Hemi Taylor, born 1964:
Welsh rugby international.

NAIROBI (Kenya)

Peter Hain, born 1950: Labour
MP for Neath and junior
Government minister.

NEW YORK CITY (USA)

Joseph Clancy, born 1928:
Poet and translator.

PONTIAC (USA)

Phyllis Kinney, born 1922:
Welsh folk singer: wife of
Maredudd Evans (qv).

PRETORIA (South Africa)

Glynis Johns, born 1928:
Leading actress:
Hollywood Oscar
Nomination for Best
Supporting Actress 1960:
Daughter of Mervyn Johns
(qv.).

ST KITTS (West Indies)

Pat Thomas, born 1950:
Cardiff-based champion
welterweight and light
middleweight boxer.

TRELEW (Argentina)

Elvey Macdonald, born 1941:
Senior administrator, Urdd
Gobaith Cymru.

TRISTAN DA CUNHA (South Atlantic)

Tristan Jones, 1924-1995,
(Born at sea off the island):
Sailor and award-winning
author.

PERSONAL NAME INDEX

Bedloe, William: Chepstow.
Bell, Richard: Penderyn.
Bell, Sir Idris: Epworth,
  Lincolnshire.
Benjamin, Bill: Shirenewton.
Bennett, Gilbert: Swansea.
Bennett, Hywel: Garnant.
Bennett, Mark: Blackwood.
Bennett, Phil: Felinfoel.
Bergiers, Roy: Carmarthen.
Berry, Henry Seymour (Lord
  Buckland): Merthyr Tydfil.
Berry, James Gomer (Lord
  Kemsley): Merthyr Tydfil.
Berry, Robert Griffith: Llanrwst.
Berry, Ron: Blaencwm.
Berry, William Ewart (Lord
  Camrose): Merthyr Tydfil.
Betts, Clive: Southampton,
  Hampshire.
Bevan, Aneurin: Tredegar.
Bevan, Bridget: Carmarthen.
Bevan, C.W.L. (Bill): London.
Bevan, John: Tylorstown.
Bevan, Percy Archibald Thomas:
  Abertillery.
Bevan, Teleri: Aberystwyth.
Bevan, Tudor: Treherbert.
Bevan, W. Derek: Clydach.
Beynon, Bill: Taibach.
Beynon, Sir Granville: Dunvant.
Bidgood, Ruth: Seven Sisters.
Bielski, Alison: Newport.
Biggs, Selwyn: Cardiff.
Birks, Frederick: Buckley.
Bishop, Walter (Waldini): Cardiff.
Blake, Nathan: Newport.
Blyth, Roger: Swansea.
Boddington, Lewis: Brithdir.
Bogdanov, Michael: Neath.
Bohana, Roy: Caernarfon.
Boon, Ronnie: Barry.
Boots, George: Aberbeeg.
Bosse-Griffiths, Kate: Wittenberg-
  am-Elbe, Germany.

Boston, Billy: Cardiff.
Boucher, Arthur: Gobowen.
Bowcott, Harry: Cardiff.
Bowden, Herbert (Lord
  Aylestone): Cardiff.
Bowen, Bleddyn: Trebanos.
Bowen, Dave: Nantyffyllon.
Bowen, David Quentin: Llanelli.
Bowen, Edward Ernest: Chepstow.
Bowen, Emrys George:
  Carmarthen.
Bowen, Euros: Treorchy.
Bowen, Geraint: Llanelli.
Bowen, Jeremy: Cardiff.
Bowen, Roderick: Cardigan.
Bowyer, Gwilym:
  Rhosllanerchrugog.
Boyce, Max: Glynneath.
Boyer, Hydwedd: Alltwen.
Brace, Sir Ivor: Abertillery.
Brace, Onllwyn: Gowerton.
Brace, Steve: Bridgend.
Brace, William: Risca.
Bradfield, James Dean: Blackwood.
Brecon, Lord (see, Lewis, David
  Vivian Penrose).
Brayley, Desmond (Lord):
  Pontypridd.
Brangwyn, Sir Frank:
  Brugge/Bruges, Belgium.
Brereton, Melissa: Mold.
Brewer, Trevor: Newport.
Brice, Siân: Porthmadog.
Brockereton, Leonard Walter:
  Cardiff.
Brockway, John: Newport.
Brooks, Beata: Abergele.
Brooks, Jack (Lord Brooks of
  Tremorfa): Cardiff.
Broome, David: Cardiff.
Broughton, Rhoda: Denbigh.
Bruce, H.A. (Lord Aberdare):
  Aberdare.
Brunt, Sir David: Staylittle.

Bryn-Jones, Delme: Cefneithin.
Buckley, William: Llanfechell.
Bufton, Sidney Osborne:
    Llandrindod Wells.
Bunford, Huw (Bunf): Cardiff.
Burcher, David: Newport.
Burne-Jones, Sir Edward:
    Birmingham.
Burnett, Ritchie: Cwmparc.
Burnett, Roy: Abercarn.
Burns, Dave: Cardiff.
Burrows, Stuart: Cilfynydd.
Burton, Charles: Treherbert.
Burton, Ian Hamilton: Pennal.
Burton, Philip: Mountain Ash.
Burton, Richard: Pontrhydyfen.
Bush, Duncan: Cardiff.
Bush, Percy: Cardiff.
Bute, 2nd Marquis of (John
    Stuart): Mount Stuart, Scotland.
Bute, 3rd Marquis of (John
    Patrick Crichton Stuart):
    Mount Stuart, Scotland.
Butler, Eddie: Newport.
Butler, Eleanor: Kilkenny, Ireland.
Button, Sir Thomas: St Nicholas.
Bye, Robert: Pontypridd.
Byles, Edward: Cwm.

C

Cable, Stuart: Cwmaman.
Cadwaladr, Betsi (Elizabeth
    Davies): Bala.
Cadwaladr, Dilys: Four Crosses.
Cadwaladr, Roger: Stretton
    Sugwas, Hereford and
    Worcester.
Cale, John: Garnant.
Callaghan, James (Lord
    Callaghan of Cardiff):
    Portsmouth, Hampshire.
Callaghan, Leo: Merthyr Tydfil.
Callice, John: Tintern.
Calvin, Wyn: Narberth.

Calzaghe, Joe: London.
Campbell, Bryn: Penrhiwceiber.
Carlile, Alex: Rossett.
Carne, Sir Edward: Nash.
Carr, William Lascelles:
    Knottingley.
Casson, Sir Lewis: Ffestiniog.
Catherine (Katrin) of Berain:
    Berain.
Cellan-Jones, Allan James:
    Swansea.
Cemlyn-Jones, Sir Wynne:
    Penmaenmawr.
Chamberlain, Brenda: Bangor.
Chambers, John Graham: Llanelli.
Chance, Thomas William: Erwood.
Chandler, Wayne: Pontypridd.
Chapman, Edward Thomas:
    Pontlottyn.
Chapman, George: London.
Charles, David: Llanfihangel
    Abercerwyn.
Charles, Jeremy: Swansea.
Charles, John: Swansea.
Charles, Mel: Swansea.
Charles, Thomas: St Clears.
Charvis, Colin: Sutton Coldfield.
Chater, Eos: Cardiff.
Childs, Euros: Carmarthen.
Childs, Megan: Carmarthen.
Chilton, Irma: Loughor.
Chinn, Nicky: Dinas Powys.
Church, Charlotte: Cardiff.
Clancy, Joseph: New York, USA.
Clay, J.C.: Bonvilston.
Clay-Jones, David: Cardigan.
Cleaver, Emrys: Llanelli.
Cleaver, W.J. (Billy): Treorchy.
Clement, Bill: Llanelli.
Clement, Tony: Swansea.
Clift, Phil: Usk.
Clift, Robert: Newport.
Clough, Sir Richard: Denbigh.
Clowes, Carl: Manchester.
Clwyd, Ann: Halkyn.

Clynnog, Morys: Clynnog Fawr.
Cobner, Terry: Blaenavon.
Coffin, Walter: Bridgend.
Cohen, Lucy: Cardiff.
Cole, David: Merthyr Tydfil.
Coleman, David: Barry.
Coles, Charles: Cardiff.
Collins, John: Aberavon.
Condry, William: Birmingham.
Cook, A.J.: Wookey, Somerset.
Cook, John: Barry.
Coombes, Bert: Madley, Hereford and Worcester.
Cooper, Tommy: Caerphilly.
Cordell, Alexander: Colombo, Sri Lanka.
Cordle, Tony: Barbados, West Indies.
Cornish, Arthur: Cardiff.
Cory, John: Bideford, Devon.
Cory, John (father): Padstow, Cornwall.
Cory, John (son): Padstow, Cornwall.
Cory, Sir Herbert: Padstow, Cornwall.
Cottey, Philip: Swansea.
Cove, W.G.: Treherbert.
Cowen, Sir Walter Henry: Crickhowell.
Cox, Idris: Maesteg.
Cradock, Walter: Llangwm.
Crawford, Anne Hariette: Caernarfon.
Crawshay, Geoffrey: Abergavenny.
Crawshay, Richard: Normanton, West Yorkshire.
Creswell, Zoe: Rhymney.
Crews, William: Llanbradach.
Croft, Robert: Swansea.
Cronin, A.J. (Archibald Joseph): Cardross, Scotland.
Cudlipp, Hugh (Lord): Cardiff.
Cummins, Peggy: Prestatyn.

Cudlipp, Percy: Cardiff.
Cudlipp, Reginald: Cardiff.
Curran, Charles: Cardiff.
Curtis, Tony: Carmarthen.
Curvis, Brian: Swansea.
Curvis, Cliff: Swansea.
Cynan, Geraint: Cardiff.
Cynon, John Marles: Cardiff.
Cynwal, William: Ysbyty Ifan.

D

Dacey, Malcolm: Swansea.
Dafis, Cynog: Swansea.
Dafydd ap Edmwnd: Hamer.
Dafydd ap Gwilym: Penrhyngoch.
Dafydd, Edward: Margam.
Dafydd Gam (Dafydd ap Llywelyn): Pen-Pont.
Dafydd, Nanmor: Nanmor.
Dagger, George: Cwmbran.
Dahl, Roald: Cardiff.
Dale, Adrian: Johannesburg, South Africa.
Dale-Jones, Don: Ruthin.
Dalton, Hugh: Neath.
Dalton, Ormonde Maddock: Cardiff.
Dalton, Timothy: Colwyn Bay.
Daniel, Glyn: Velfrey.
Daniel, Sir Goronwy Hopkin: Ystradgynlais.
Daniel, J.E.: Bangor.
Daniel, Ray: Swansea.
Darren, John: Mountain Ash.
Davey, Claude: Garnant.
Davey, David Garnet: Caerphilly.
David, Saint: St Bride's Bay.
David, Dennis 'Hurricane': Tongwynlais.
David, Sir Edgeworth: St Fagans.
David, Hugh: Cardiff.
David, Tom: Pontypridd.
David, Wayne: Bridgend.
Davidge, Glyn: Newport.

113

Davies, Adrian: Carmarthen.
Davies, Alfred: Blaengarw.
Davies, Sir Alun Talfan: Gorseinon.
Davies, Andrew: Cardiff.
Davies, Aneurin Talfan: Felindre.
Davies, Arthur: Merthyr Tydfil.
Davies, Sir Arthur: Barry.
Davies, Ben: Dinas.
Davies, Ben: Pontardawe.
Davies, Bryan Martin: Brynaman.
Davies, Bryn: Tonyrefail.
Davies, Clara Novello: Cardiff.
Davies, Clement: Llanfyllin.
Davies, Cuthbert Collin: Narberth.
Davies, Dai (footballer): Ammanford.
Davies, Dai (cricketer): Llanelli.
Davies, Sir Daniel: Pontycymmer.
Davies, David (geologist): Gilfach Goch.
Davies, David: Llandinam.
Davies, David (Lord Davies of Llandinam): Llandinam.
Davies, David (journalist): Llanelli.
Davies, David (Dai'r Cantwr): Llancarfan.
Davies, Sir David (trade unionist): Ebbw Vale.
Davies, Sir David (royal physician): Llanddewi Brefi.
Davies, Sir David (tourism): Maesteg.
Davies, David Christopher: Oswestry, Shropshire.
Davies, David Richard: Pwllheli.
Davies, David Vaughan: Cemaes.
Davies, Denzil: Carmarthen.
Davies, Desmond: Pentlepoir.
Davies, E.T.: Dowlais.
Davies, E. Tegla: Llandegla.
Davies, Ednyfed Hudson: Kidwelly.
Davies, Elwyn: Llandeilo.

Davies, Emlyn Glyndwr: Bargoed.
Davies, Emrys: Llanelli.
Davies, Eryl Oliver: Merthyr Tydfil.
Davies, Evan (Myfyr Morganwg): Pencoed.
Davies, Evan Thomas: Dowlais.
Davies, Gareth Alban: Ton Pentre.
Davies, Garfield: Bridgend.
Davies, Geraint Glynne: Llanrwst.
Davies, Geraint Talfan: Carmarthen.
Davies, Gerald: Llansaint.
Davies, Gilli: Sleaford, Lincolnshire.
Davies, Glyn: Cilfynydd.
Davies, Griffith: Llandwrog.
Davies, Gwendoline: Llandinam.
Davies, Gwilym: Bedlinog.
Davies, Gwilym Elfed (Lord Davies of Penrhys): Tylorstown.
Davies, Haydn (politician): Aberystwyth.
Davies, Haydn (cricketer): Llanelli.
Davies, Herbert Edmund (Lord Edmund-Davies of Aberpennar): Mountain Ash.
Davies, Howell: Pyle.
Davies, Hugh Humphreys: Llangynog.
Davies, Hywel (jockey): Cardigan.
Davies, Hywel (BBC): Llandyssul.
Davies, Idris: Rhymney.
Davies, Ifor (MP): Gowerton.
Davies, Ifor (painter): Treharris.
Davies, Iforwyn Glyndwr: Porth.
Davies, Ithel: Llanbrynmair.
Davies, James Eirian: Nantgaredig.
Davies, James: Wyndham.
Davies, James Kitchener: Cors Caron.
Davies, Jenkin Alban: London.
Davies, John (WEA): Blaenpennal.
Davies, John (poet): Cymer Afan.

Davies, John (poet): Hereford, Hereford and Worcester.

Davies, John (scholar): Llanferres.

Davies, John (family bard): Llanuwchllyn).

Davies, John (missionary): Pontrobert.

Davies, John (athlete): Llwynypia.

Davies, John (historian): Llwynypia.

Davies, John Cadfan: Llangadfan.

Davies, John Haydn: Blaencwm.

Davies, Jonathan: Trimsaran.

Davies, Lilian: Cardiff.

Davies, Lyn: Nantymoel.

Davies, Maldwyn Thomas: Rhigos.

Davies, Mansel: Aberdare.

Davies, Margaret: Llandinam.

Davies, Mark: Maesteg.

Davies, Mary: London.

Davies, Mervyn: Swansea.

Davies, Mike: Swansea.

Davies, Neil: Burry Port.

Davies Nigel: Glanaman.

Davies, Ogwyn: Trebanos.

Davies, Pennar: Mountain Ash.

Davies, Phil: Seven Sisters.

Davies, Rhoslyn: Treorchy.

Davies, Rhys (writer): Blaenclydach.

Davies, Rhys (MP): Llangennech.

Davies, Richard (bishop): Conwy.

Davies, Richard (MP): Llangefni.

Davies, Richard (Quaker): Welshpool.

Davies, Robert: Nantyglyn.

Davies, Ron: Machen.

Davies, Ryan: Llanaman.

Davies, Ryland: Cwm.

Davies, S.O. (Stephen Owen): Abercwmboi.

Davies, T. Glynne: Llanrwst.

Davies, Terry: Llwynhendy.

Davies, Tom: Pontypridd.

Davies, W.H.: Newport.

Davies, Sir Walford: Oswestry, Shropshire.

Davies, Walter (Gwallter Mechain): Llanfechain.

Davies, William (martyr): Croes-yr-eirias.

Davies, William (palaeontologist): Holywell.

Davies, William (musician): Rhosllanerchrugog.

Davies, Sir William (librarian): Pwllheli.

Davies, Sir William (journalist): Talley.

Davies, William John: Carmarthen.

Davies, William John Abbott: Pembroke Dock.

Davies, Windsor: London.

Davies, Wyndham Roy: Llangadog.

Davis, Sir Charles Thomas: Brecon.

Davis, Roger: Cardiff.

Davis, William: Wrexham.

Dawes, John: Newbridge.

Dawkins, Sir William Boyd: Buttington.

Dee, John: London.

Deiniol, Father: Blaenau Ffestiniog.

Deio ap Ieuan Du: Creuddyn.

De Lloyd, David: Skewen.

Deniz, Jose (Joe): Cardiff.

Dennis, Henry: Bodmin, Cornwall.

Derfel, Robert James: Llandderfel.

Devereux, John: Pontycymmer.

De Winton, Wilfred Seymour: Brecon.

Dickie, Robert: Carmarthen.

Dillwyn, Elizabeth Amy: Swansea.

Dillwyn, Llewellyn John: Pennllergaer.

Disley, John: Corris.

Dodd, A.H.: Wrexham.

Dodd, Francis: Holyhead.

Dodd, Stephen: Barry.
Donner, Richard: Eastwood,
Nottinghamshire.
Doughty, Neale: Kenfig Hill.
Doyle, Mike: Carmarthen.
Driscoll, Jim: Cardiff.
Duncan, Sir David: Penarth.
Duncan, Tony: Cardiff.
Durban, Allan: Port Talbot.
Dwnn, Lewis (Lewis ap Rhys ab
Owen): Betws Cedewain.
Dyer, John: Llanfynydd.
Dyson, Arnold: Halifax, West
Yorkshire.

E

Eames, Aled: Llandudno.
Eames, Marion: Birkenhead,
Cheshire.
Earle, Jean: Bristol.
Earley, Tom: Mountain Ash.
Ebenezer, Lyn: Pontrhydfendigaid.
Edelman, Maurice: Cardiff.
Edward II: Caernarfon.
Edwards, Sir Charles: Risca.
Edwards, Charles Alfred:
Kitchener, Canada.
Edwards, Dorothy: Ogmore Vale.
Edwards, Gareth: Gwaun-Cae-
Gurwen.
Edwards, George Alfred: Llan-
ym-mawddwy.
Edwards, Gwynne: Tonypandy.
Edwards, Harold: Newport.
Edwards, Huw: Bridgend.
Edwards, Huw Lloyd: Deiniolen.
Edwards, Huw T.: Rowen.
Edwards, Hywel Teifi: Llanddewi
Aber-arth.
Edwards, Sir Ifan ab Owen:
Llanuwchllyn.
Edwards, Ifor Prys: Aberystwyth.
Edwards, Iorwerth Eiddon
Stephen: London.

Edwards, J.M.: Llanrhysted.
Edwards, John (Siôn Treredyn):
Caldicot.
Edwards, Sir John Goronwy:
Manchester.
Edwards, Lewis: Pen-y-banc.
Edwards, Maudie: Neath.
Edwards, Meirion: Port Dinorwic.
Edwards, Meredith:
Rhosllanerchrugog.
Edwards, Morgan: Pontypool.
Edwards, Ness: Abertillery.
Edwards, Noreen: Pentir.
Edwards, Owen: Aberystwyth.
Edwards, Owen Morys:
Llanuwchllyn.
Edwards, Prys: Aberystwyth.
Edwards, Raymond:
Rhosllanerchrogog.
Edwards, Richey: Blackwood.
Edwards, Thomas (Twm o'r
Nant): Llannefydd.
Edwards, Thomas Charles: Bala.
Edwards, Tracy: Swansea.
Egerton, Sir Alfred Charles Glyn:
Talsarnau.
Eidman, Ian: Cardiff.
Elias, John (Brynllwyn Bach):
Pwllheli.
Elis, Islwyn Ffowc: Wrexham.
Elis, Richard: Ammanford.
Elis-Thomas, Dafydd (Lord):
Llanrwst.
Ellice, Robert: Bersham.
Ellis, Alice Thomas: Liverpool.
Ellis, Huw: Trawsfynydd.
Ellis, Osian: Ffynnongroew.
Ellis, Rowland: Penrhos.
Ellis, Ruth: Rhyl.
Ellis, Lady Ruth: Liverpool.
Ellis, Thomas E.: Cefnddwysarn.
Ellis, Thomas Iorwerth: London.
Elwyn, John: Adpar.
Elwyn-Jones, Frederick (Lord):
See Jones, Frederick Elwyn.

Elyston-Morgan, Dafydd (Lord):
Aberystwyth.
Emlyn, Endaf: Pwllheli.
Emanual, David: Bridgend.
Emmanuel, Ivor: Pontrhydyfen.
Emrys-Roberts, Kenyon: Penarth.
Emrys, Arthur: Bangor.
England, Mike: Greenfield.
Erskine, Joe: Cardiff.
Etheridge, Ken: Ammanford.
Evans, Alan: Ferndale.
Evans, Ann: London.
Evans, Ann Catrin: Bethesda.
Evans, Beriah Gwynfe: Nantyglo.
Evans, Caradoc: Llanfihangel-yr-
arth.
Evans, Sir Charles: Corwen.
Evans, Christopher: Port Talbot.
Evans, Clifford: Llanelli.
Evans, Daniel Silvan: Llanarth.
Evans, David (Lord Evans of
Claughton): Birkenhead,
Cheshire.
Evans, David (Samaritans):
Llanglydwen.
Evans, David (musician): Resolven.
Evans, David Ellis: Llanfynydd.
Evans, David Emlyn: Newcastle
Emlyn.
Evans, David Gwilym Lloyd:
London.
Evans, David Lewis: Bridgend.
Evans, David Owen: Llandovery.
Evans, David Philip: Port Talbot.
Evans, David Traherne: Llantrisant.
Evans, E. Eynon: Nelson.
Evans, Edgar: Rhosili.
Evans, Elis Humphrey (Hedd
Wyn): Trawsfynydd.
Evans, Ellen: Pentre.
Evans, Emrys: Llanfair Careinion.
Evans, Emyr Estyn: Welshpool.
Evans, Eric (education): Lampeter.
Evans, Eric (rugby): Neath.
Evans, Evan: Llanrhystud.

Evans, Evan (Ieuan Fardd):
Lledrod.
Evans, Evan (Ieuan Glan
Geirionydd): Trefriw.
Evans, Evan Gwyndaf:
Llanfachreth.
Evans, Fred: Aberfan.
Evans, George Ewart: Abercynon.
Evans, Sir Geraint: Cilfynydd.
Evans, Griffith: Tywyn.
Evans, Gwyn: Maesteg.
Evans, Gwynfor: Barry.
Evans, Harry: Dowlais.
Evans, Howell Thomas:
Cwmbwrla.
Evans, Hugh Garner: Llangollen.
Evans, Sir Hywel Wynn:
Liverpool.
Evans, Idris: Ammanford.
Evans, Ieuan: Capel Dewi.
Evans, Ifor Leslie: Aberdare.
Evans, Ioan: Llanelli.
Evans, John (preacher): Abererch.
Evans, John (MP): Cwmparc.
Evans, John (Y Bardd Cocos):
Menai Bridge.
Evans, John (rugby): Newbridge.
Evans, John (explorer): Waunfawr.
Evans, John Gwenogvryn:
Llanybyther.
Evans, John Young: Aberystwyth.
Evans, Lee: Rhyl.
Evans, Lewis: Caerleon.
Evans, Lewis Pugh: Aberystwyth.
Evans, Sir Lincoln: Swansea.
Evans, Linda: Briton Ferry.
Evans, Maureen: Cardiff.
Evans, Maredudd: Llanegryn.
Evans, Margiad: London.
Evans, Meirion William:
Llanfihangel-y-pennant.
Evans, Merlyn Oliver: Cardiff.
Evans, Mostyn (Moss): Merthyr
Tydfil.
Evans, Nick: Newport.

Evans, Philip: Monmouth.
Evans, Rebecca: Pontrhydyfen.
Evans, Rhydwen Harding: Pontarddulais.
Evans, Rhys (Arise): Llangelynnion.
Evans, Roy: Gorseinon.
Evans, Samuel: Ruabon.
Evans, Sir Samuel: Skewen.
Evans, Stuart (rugby): Neath.
Evans, Stuart (writer): Swansea.
Evans, Theophilus: Newcastle Emlyn.
Evans, Thomas (Tomos Glyn Cothi): Gwernogle.
Evans, Thomas Hopkin: Resolven.
Evans, Timothy John: Merthyr Vale.
Evans, Sir Vincent: Llangelynin.
Evans, William (grocery chain): Fishguard.
Evans, William (cardiologist): Tregaron.
Evans, William (Wil Ifan): Llanwinio.
Evans, William Davies: St Dogwell's.
Evans, William Emrys: Llangadfan.
Evans Bevan, Sir David: Cadoxton-juxta-Neath.
Evans-Jones, Sir Albert (Cynan): Pwllheli.
Evans-Thomas, Sir Hugh: Neath.
Everest, Sir George: Gwernvale.
Everson, Bill: Newport.

F

Farr, Tommy: Clydach Vale.
Felton, Roland Oliver: Port Talbot.
Fenton, Sir Richard: St David's.
Fenwick, Steve: Nantgarw.
Ferris, Paul: Swansea.
Ffangcon-Davies, Dame Gwen: London.

Finch, Peter: Cardiff.
Fisher, George: Bargoed.
Fishlock, Trevor: Hereford, Hereford and Worcester.
Flook, Brian: Newport.
Flynn, Brian: Port Talbot.
Flynn, Paul: Cardiff.
Follett, Ken: Cardiff.
Ford, Trevor: Swansea.
Foster, Sir Idris: Bethesda.
Fothergill, Richard: Kendal, Cumbria.
Foulkes, Isaac: Llanfwrog.
Fox, Sir Cyril: Chippenham, Wiltshire.
Francis, Albert: Liverpool.
Francis, Dai: Onllwyn.
Francis, Dick: Tenby.
Francis, Hywel: Onllwyn.
Francis, J.O.: Merthyr Tydfil.
Freeman, Kathleen: Cardiff.
French, Dawn: Holyhead.
Frere, Sir Bartle: Brynmawr.
Frost, Bill: Saundersfoot.
Frost, John: Newport.
Fuller, William: Laugharne.

G

Gabe, Rhys: Llangennech.
Gale, Norman: Gorseinon.
Gallie, Menna: Ystradgynlais.
Gambould, William: Cardigan.
Garel-Jones, Tristan (Lord): Gorseinon.
Garlick, Raymond: London.
Gee, Thomas: Denbigh.
Geoffrey of Monmouth: Monmouth.
George, David Lloyd (Earl of Dwyfor): Manchester.
George, Gwilym Lloyd (Lord Tenby): Criccieth.
George, Megan Lloyd (Lady): Criccieth.

George, Siwsann: Church Village.
George, William (poet): Criccieth.
George, William (solicitor):
    Llanystumdwy.
Gerald of Wales: Manorbier.
Giardelli, Arthur: London.
Gibbs, Scott: Bridgend.
Gibson, John: Conwy.
Gibson-Watt, David (Lord):
    Llandrindod Wells.
Giggs, Ryan: Cardiff.
Gildas: 'The Old North'.
Gittins, Charles Edward:
    Rhostyllen.
Gittins, John: Welshpool.
Glendenning, Raymond: Newport.
Glenton, Robert: Porthcawl.
Goodman, John: Bangor.
Goodwin, Geraint:
    Llanllwchhaearn.
Gordon, Sir Alex: Ayr.
Gough, Matthew: Maelor.
Gould, Arthur (Monkey): Newport.
Gower, Idris: Swansea.
Gower, Sir Raymond: Cardiff.
Gravell, Ray: Kidwelly.
Gray, Tim: Abercynon.
Green, Charles Alfred: Llanelli.
Greenaway, Frank: Cardiff.
Greenslade, Edwin (Ned):
    Pontycymmer.
Grenfell, David (Dai): Swansea.
Grey, Nixon (David McNeil):
    Cardiff.
Grey, Tanni: Cardiff.
Griffith, David (Clwydfardd):
    Denbigh.
Griffith, Hugh: Marian Glas.
Griffith, John: Barmouth.
Griffith, John: Rhyl.
Griffith, Kenneth: Tenby.
Griffith, Llewellyn Wyn: Dolgellau.
Griffith, Moses: Bryncroes.
Griffith, Sir Samuel: Merthyr Tydfil.
Griffith-Boscawen, Sir Arthur:
    Wrexham.

Griffiths, Ann (harpist): Cwmgors.
Griffiths, Ann (hymnwriter):
    Llanfihangel-yng-ngwynfa.
Griffiths, Arfon: Wrexham.
Griffiths, Bryn: Swansea.
Griffiths, Ernest Howard: Brecon.
Griffiths, Gareth: Penygraig.
Griffiths, James: Llanelli.
Griffiths, John: Treharris.
Griffiths, John Gwyn: Porth.
Griffiths, Mervyn: Abertillery.
Griffiths, Mike: Tonypandy.
Griffiths, Milo: Crymmych.
Griffiths, Philip Jones: Rhuddlan.
Griffiths, Ralph: Aberbargoed.
Griffiths, Richard: Llanwonno.
Griffiths, Roy: Welshpool.
Griffiths, Terry: Llanelli.
Griffiths, Walter: Newport.
Griffiths, Winston:
    Grahamstown, South Africa.
Grimes, William: Pembroke Dock.
Gruffudd ap Yr Unad Goch:
    Llanddyfnan.
Gruffudd Grug: Llantrisant.
Gruffudd, Heini: Dolgellau.
Gruffudd, Hiraethog: Llangollen.
Gruffudd, Ioan: Cardiff.
Gruffudd, Robat: Llwynypia.
Gruffydd ap Cynan: Dublin,
    Ireland.
Gruffydd, Ellis: Llanasa.
Gruffydd, Geraint: Talybont.
Gruffydd, Ifan: Llangristiolus.
Gruffydd, William John: Bethel.
Gubay, Albert: Rhyl.
Guest, Lady Charlotte: Uffington,
    Lincolnshire.
Guest, George Hywel: Bangor.
Guest, Sir Josiah John: Dowlais.
Gummer, Selwyn: Blaengarw.
Gunter, Ray: Llanhilleth.
Gunter, William: Raglan.
Guto'r, Glyn: Glynceiriog.

Gutun Owain: Oswestry, Shropshire.
Guy, Alun: Cardiff.
Guy, Sir Henry Lewis: Penarth.
Gwalchmai ap Meilyr: Trewalchmai.
Gwerful Mechain: Llansantffraid-ym-mechain.
Gwilliam, John: Pontypridd.
Gwyn ap Gwilym: Bangor.
Gwyn, Richard: Llanidloes.
Gwyn, Harri: Swansea.
Gwynfryn, Hywel: Llangefni.
Gwynn, Robert: Penyberth.
Gwynne, Howell Arthur: Swansea.

H

Haddock, Neil: Llanelli.
Hadley, Adrian: Cardiff.
Hain, Peter: Nairobi, Kenya.
Hall, Augusta (Lady Llanover): Llanover Hall.
Hall, Benjamin: Llandaff.
Hall, Sir Benjamin: Hensol Castle.
Hall, George (1st Viscount of Cynon Valley): Penrhiwceiber.
Hall, Ian: Gilfach Goch.
Hall, Leonard (2nd Viscount of Cynon Valley): Ynysybwl.
Hall, Mike: Bridgend.
Hallam, Chris: Cwmbran.
Hamilton, John Hussey (Lord Swansea): Builth Wells.
Hancock, Fred: Wiveliscome, Somerset.
Hanley, James: Liverpool.
Hanmer, Sir Thomas (horticulturalist): Bettisfield Park.
Hanmer, Sir Thomas (Speaker): Bettisfield Park.
Hannon, Daniel: Rotherham, South Yorkshire.

Harcombe, Mark: Cwmavon.
Hardie, Keir: Holytown, Scotland.
Harding, Lyn: St Bride's Wentloog.
Harding, Rowe: Swansea.
Hare, Doris: Bargoed.
Harrhy, Eiddwen, Swansea.
Harries, Rhys: Newbridge.
Harrington, Alan: Cogan.
Harrington, Illtyd: Merthyr Tydfil.
Harris, Howell: Trefeca.
Harris, Joseph (Gomer): Llantydewi.
Harris, Oliver: Sirhowy.
Harris, Peter: Swansea.
Hartshorn, Vernon: Pontywaun.
Havard, Floyd: Clydach.
Haycock, Myfanwy: Pontnewynydd.
Hayward, David (Dai): Crumlin.
Healy, Linda: Welshpool.
Hedges, Bernard: Pontypridd.
Hellings, Dick: Tiverton, Devon.
Hemens, Felicia Dorothea: Liverpool.
Hennessey, Terry: Llay.
Hennessy, Frank: Cardiff.
Henry V: Monmouth.
Henry VII: Pembroke.
Herbert, George: Montgomery.
Heseltine, Michael: Swansea.
Heseltine, Nigel: Montgomery.
Hewitt, Ron: Flint.
Heycock, Clayton: Port Talbot.
Heycock, Llewellyn (Lord Heycock of Taibach): Port Talbot.
Hislop, Ian: Mumbles.
Hoddinott, Alun: Bargoed.
Hodge, Cyril: Cardiff.
Hodge, Sir Julian: London.
Hodges, Frank: Blaengarw.
Hodges, Glyn: London.
Hodgson, Grahame: Ogmore Vale.
Hogg, A.H.A.: London.
Hole, Barry: Swansea.

Holland, Hugh: Denbigh.
Holland, Robert: Conwy.
Holmes, Terry: Cardiff.
Hooson, Emlyn (Lord): Denbigh.
Hooson, Tom Ellis: Denbigh.
Hopkin, Mary: Pontardawe.
Hopkins, Sir Anthony: Taibach.
Hopkins, Gerald Manley:
   London.
Hopkins, John: Maesteg.
Hopkins, Ted: Neath.
Hopkyn, Will: Llangynwyd.
Horne, Barry: St Asaph.
Horner, Arthur: Aberdare.
Houston, Donald: Tonypandy.
Houston, Glyn: Tonypandy.
Howard, Michael: Gorseinon.
Howe, Geoffrey (Lord Howe of
   Aberavon): Port Talbot.
Howell, Catrin: Newcastle Emlyn.
Howell, Gwynne: Gorseinon.
Howell, James: Abernant.
Howell, Lyn: Aberdulais.
Howells, Anne: Southport,
   Lancashire.
Howells, Geraint (Lord Geraint
   of Ponterwyd): Ponterwyd.
Howells, Jack: Abertysswg.
Howells, Kim: Merthyr Tydfil.
Howley, Robert: Bridgend.
Hoyle, William Evans: Manchester.
Hudson-Williams, Thomas:
   Caernarfon.
Huggett, Brian: Porthcawl.
Hughes, Annie Harriet: Talsarnau.
Hughes, Arwel: Rhosllanerchrgog.
Hughes, Beti: St Clears.
Hughes, Cledwyn: Llansantffraed.
Hughes, Lord Cledwyn of
   Penrhos: Holyhead.
Hughes, Dafydd: Aberystwyth.
Hughes, Edward Davies: Criccieth.
Hughes, Edward Ernest: Tywyn.
Hughes, Emrys: Tonypandy.

Hughes, Ezeckiel: Llanbrynmair.
Hughes, Glyn Tegai: Newtown.
Hughes, Gwilym Rees: Llanllechid.
Hughes, Hugh (artist): Llandudno.
Hughes, Hugh (Welsh language):
   Llandyfrdog.
Hughes, Hywel: Mold.
Hughes, John (ironmaster):
   Merthyr Tydfil.
Hughes, John (journalist): Neath.
Hughes, John (potter): Pontypridd.
Hughes, John Ceiriog: Llanarmon.
Hughes, John L.: Pontypridd.
Hughes, Jonathan: Llangollen.
Hughes, Joshua: Nevern.
Hughes, Margaret (Lelia
   Megane): Bethesda.
Hughes, Mark: Rhosllanerchrugog.
Hughes, Moelwyn: Cardigan.
Hughes, Nerys: Rhyl.
Hughes, Owain Arwel: Ton Pentre.
Hughes Richard: Weybridge,
   Surrey.
Hughes, Ronnie, Aberystwyth.
Hughes, Roy (Lord Islwyn of
   Casnewydd): Pontllanfraith.
Hughes, Stephen: Carmarthen.
Hughes, T. Rowland: Llanberis.
Hughes, Sir Thomas John:
   Bridgend.
Hughes, William (Billy):
   Llandudno.
Humphrey, John Basson:
   Newtown.
Humphreys, Beverley: Bedwas.
Humphreys, Edward Morgan:
   Dyffryn Ardudwy.
Humphreys, John: Cardiff.
Humphreys, John: North Cornelly.
Humphreys-Owen, Arthur:
   Garthmyl.
Humphries, Emyr: Prestatyn.
Humphries, Humphrey:
   Penrhyndeudraeth.

121

Humphries, John: Newport.
Huws, Llyfni: Penygroes.
Hywel, Dafydd: Glanaman.

I

Ieuan, Dafydd: Bangor.
Ifor Bach (Ifor ap Meurig):
    Senghenydd.
Ifor Hael (Ifor ap Llywelyn):
    Bassaleg.
Ignatius, Father: London.
Innes, James Dickson: Llanelli.
Insole, James Harvey: Leicester,
    Leicestershire.
Ioan, Gareth: Abergynolwen.
Iorwerth Fynglwyd: St Brides
    Major.
Iwan, Dafydd: Brynaman.

J

Jackson, Sir Charles James:
    Monmouth.
Jackson, Colin: Cardiff.
Jacobs, David Henry: Cardiff.
Jacobs, Sarah: Llanfihangel
    Iorarth.
James, Arthur Lloyd:
    Penrhiwceiber.
James, Basil: Gwaelod-y-garth.
James, Carwyn: Cefneithen.
James, D.G.: Griffithstown.
James, Sir David: London.
James, David Emrys: Newquay.
James, David William Francis:
    Merthyr Tydfil.
James, Evan (composer):
    Caerphilly.
James, Evan (rugby): Swansea.
James, Gerald: Brecon.
James, James (composer):
    Bedwellty.
James, James (rugby): Swansea.
James, Jenkin: Llanarth.
James, Leighton: Loughor.
James, Richard: Carmarthen.

James, Robbie: Gorseinon.
James, Ronnie: Pontardawe.
James, Shani Rhys: Melbourne,
    Australia.
James, Siân (novelist): Llandyssul.
James, Siân (singer): Llanerfyl.
James, Stephen: Lydney,
    Gloucerthshire.
James, Thomas: Llanddewi Skirrid.
James, Thomas Henry: Neath.
James, Wayne: Tredegar.
Janes, Alfred: Swansea.
Janner, Barnett: Barry.
Jarman, Alfred Owen Hughes:
    Bangor.
Jarman, Geraint: Denbigh.
Jarrett, Keith: Newport.
Jarvis, Lee: Pontypridd.
Jeffreys, George (Lord): Wrexham.
Jeffreys-Jones, Thomas Ieuan:
    Rhymney.
Jenkins, Arthur: Varteg.
Jenkins, Clive: Port Talbot.
Jenkins, Clive Ferguson: Swansea.
Jenkins, Dafydd: London.
Jenkins, David (librarian):
    Blaenclydach.
Jenkins, David (TUC): Cardiff.
Jenkins, David (royalist): Hensol
    Castle.
Jenkins, David (composer):
    Trecastle.
Jenkins, Emyr: Machynlleth.
Jenkins, Garin: Ynysbwl.
Jenkins, Geraint Huw:
    Aberystwyth.
Jenkins, Helen: Newbridge.
Jenkins, John (Gwili): Hendy.
Jenkins, John (Ifor Ceri):
    Llangoedmor.
Jenkins, John Geraint:
    Llangrannog.
Jenkins, Karl: Penclawdd.
Jenkins, Leighton: Tredegar.
Jenkins, Sir Leoline: Llanblethian.

Jenkins, Neil: Pontypridd.
Jenkins, Nigel: Gorseinon.
Jenkins, R.T.: Manchester.
Jenkins, Rae: Ammanford.
Jenkins, Roy (Lord Jenkins of
    Hillhead): Abersychan.
Jenkins, Tom: Port Talbot.
Jenkins, Vivian: Port Talbot.
Jenkins, Sir William: Cymer Afan.
Job, John Thomas: Llandybie.
John ap John: Ruabon.
John, Augustus: Tenby.
John, Barry: Cefneithen.
John, Brynmor: Pontypridd.
John, David Dilwyn: Llangan.
John, Edward Thomas:
    Pontypridd.
John, Gwen: Haverfordwest.
John, Roy: Neath.
John, Thomas: Llantrithyd.
John, Thomas George: Pembroke
    Dock.
John, Will: Cockett.
John, Sir William Goscombe:
    Llandaff.
Johnes, Arthur James: Garthmyl.
Johnes, Thomas: Ludlow,
    Shropshire.
Johns, Glynis: Pretoria, South
    Africa.
Johns, Mervyn: Pembroke.
Johnson, Hubert: Cardiff.
Johnsey, Debbie: Newport.
Jones, Alan: Velindre.
Jones, Alan Lewis: Alltwen.
Jones, Aled: Llandegfan.
Jones, Alun: Trefor.
Jones, Alun Gwynne (Lord
    Chalfont): Llantarnam.
Jones, Alun Jeremiah (Alun
    Cilie): Llangrannog.
Jones, Aubrey: Merthyr Tydfil.
Jones, Barry: Cardiff.
Jones, Bedwyr Lewis: Wrexham.
Jones, Bryn: Merthyr Tydfil.
Jones, Sir Brynmor:
    Rhosllanerchrugog.

Jones, Sir Cadwaladr Bryner:
    Dolgellau.
Jones, Calvert Richard: Swansea.
Jones, Catherine Zeta: Mumbles.
Jones, Christopher: Pontypridd.
Jones, Clay (see Clay-Jones, David).
Jones, Clement: Llandrindod Wells.
Jones, Cliff (rugby): Porth.
Jones, Cliff (football): Swansea.
Jones, Clifford (Clifford Deri): Deri.
Jones, Colin: Gorseinon.
Jones, Dafydd (hymn writer):
    Cwm Gogerddan.
Jones, Dafydd (poet): Ffair Rhos.
Jones, Dan: Ynyshir.
Jones, Daniel: Pembroke.
Jones, David (swimmer): Baglan.
Jones, David (artist): Brockley,
    Kent.
Jones, David (musician):
    Carreghofa.
Jones, David (Defynnog): Libanus.
Jones, David (printer): Trefriw.
Jones, David Elwyn: Ffestiniog.
Jones, David Evan Alun:
    Aberaeron.
Jones, David Ifon: Aberystwyth.
Jones, David James (Gwenallt):
    Alltwen.
Jones, David Watkin: Merthyr
    Tydfil.
Jones, Della: Neath.
Jones, Derwyn: Pontarddulais.
Jones, Dic: Tre'r Ddol.
Jones, Dill: Newcastle Emlyn.
Jones, Dyfed Glyn: Gaerwen.
Jones, E. Alfred: Llanfyllin.
Jones, Edward: Llanelidan.
Jones, Edward (Bardd y Brenin):
    Llandderfel.
Jones, Eifion: Velindre.
Jones, Einir: Traeth Goch.
Jones, Elias Henry: Aberystwyth.
Jones, Elizabeth Mary: Rhydlewis.

Jones, Elizabeth Watkin: Nefyn.
Jones, Elwyn: Cwmaman.
Jones, Frederick Elwyn (Lord):
Llanelli.
Jones, Emrys (geographer):
Aberdare.
Jones, Emrys (cricket): Briton Ferry.
Jones, Emrys (Labour Party):
Mountain Ash.
Jones, Erasmus: Llanddeiniolen.
Jones, Eric: Tremadoc.
Jones, Ernest: Gowerton.
Jones, Eurfron Gwynne: Aberdare.
Jones, Evan: Porthmadog.
Jones, Evan (Ieuan Gwynedd):
Dolgellau.
Jones, Evan Pan: Llandyssul.
Jones, Sir Evan Davies: Fishguard.
Jones, F. Llewellyn: Penrhiwceiber.
Jones, Francis: Trevine.
Jones, Gareth: Barry.
Jones, Gareth Hywel: Tylorstown.
Jones, Geraint: Porth.
Jones, Geraint Stanley: Pontypridd.
Jones, Gerallt: Rhymney.
Jones, Glyn: Merthyr Tydfil.
Jones, Glynne: Dowlais.
Jones, Griff Rhys: Cardiff.
Jones, Griffith (Llanddowror):
Penboyr.
Jones, Griffith Hartwell:
Llanrhaeadr-ym-mochnant.
Jones, Griffith Hugh: Llanberis.
Jones, Griffith Rhys (Caradog):
Trecynon.
Jones, Gwilym R.: Tal-y-sarn.
Jones, Gwyn (scholar): Blackwood.
Jones, Gwyn (businessman):
Porthmadog.
Jones, Gwyn Erfyl: Llanerfyl.
Jones, Gwyn Hughes: Bangor.
Jones, Gwyn Owain: Cardiff.
Jones, Dame Gwyneth:
Pontnewynydd.

Jones, Gwyneth Ceris: Bangor.
Jones, Gwynoro: Cefneithen.
Jones, Harri Pritchard: Dudley,
Hereford and Worcester.
Jones, Haydn Harold: Penarth.
Jones, Heather: Cardiff.
Jones, Sir Henry: Llangernyw.
Jones, Hugh Robert: Deiniolen.
Jones, Humphrey Owen: Goginan.
Jones, Humphrey Rowland: Tre'r
Ddol.
Jones, Hywel Francis: Morriston.
Jones, Idwal (writer): Blaenau
Ffestiniog.
Jones, Idwal (playwright):
Lampeter.
Jones, Ieuan Wyn: Denbigh.
Jones, Ifano: Aberdare.
Jones, Inigo: Llanrwst.
Jones, Iolo: Plymouth, Devon.
Jones, Ivor: Loughor.
Jones, Ivor Roberts: Oswestry,
Shropshire.
Jones, J. Cynddylan: Capel Dewi.
Jones, Jack: Merthyr Tydfil.
Jones, James Idwal: Ruabon.
Jones, Jeff: Dafen.
Jones, Jenny: Pontypridd.
Jones, Joey: Llandudno.
Jones, John (penillion): Dolgellau.
Jones, John (preacher):
Dolwyddelan.
Jones, John (poet): Llanfair
Talhaearn.
Jones, John (printer):
Llansantffraed Glan Conwy.
Jones, John (colonel): Maes-y-
garnedd.
Jones, John (Jac Glan-y-gors):
Cerrig-y-drudion.
Jones, John (Shoni Sgubor Fawr):
Penderyn.
Jones, John (Talsarn): Tanycastell.
Jones, John Daniel: Ruthin.

Jones, John David Rheinallt: Llanrug.

Jones, John Gwilym: Groeslon.

Jones, John Morgan (economist): Caersws.

Jones, John Morgan (pacifist): Margam.

Jones, John Rice: Mallwyd.

Jones, John Robert: Pwllheli.

Jones, John Viriamu: Pentrepoeth.

Jones, Jonah: Durham.

Jones, Jonathan: Fishguard.

Jones, Joseph: Brecon.

Jones, Kelly: Cwmaman.

Jones, Ken: Blaenavon.

Jones, Kinglsey (rugby): Nantyglo.

Jones, Kingsley (rugby Lion): Pontypridd.

Jones, Leslie: Tumble.

Jones, Sir Lewis: Brynaman.

Jones, Lewis (Patagonia): Caernarfon.

Jones, Lewis (writer): Clydach Vale.

Jones, Lewis (rugby): Gorseinon.

Jones, Mai: Newport.

Jones, Mary: Llanfihangel-y-pennant.

Jones, Maurice: Trawsfynydd.

Jones, Mervyn (jockey): Carmarthen.

Jones, Mervyn (administrator): Llandinam.

Jones, Michael D.: Llanuwchllyn.

Jones, Morgan: Trecynon.

Jones, Nathan Rocyn: Abertillery.

Jones, Nesta Wyn: Dolgellau.

Jones, Owen: London.

Jones, Owen (Owen Myfyr): Llanfihangel Glyn Myfyr.

Jones, Owen Glynne: London.

Jones, Owen Thomas: Beulah.

Jones, Parry: Blaina.

Jones, Percy: Porth.

Jones, Rhiannon Davies: Llanbedr.

Jones, Rhydderch: Aberllefni.

Jones, Richard (Stereophonics): Cwmaman.

Jones, Richard (novelist): Rhydyfelin.

Jones, Richard Robert (Dic Aberdaron): Aberdaron.

Jones, Rita: Bargoed.

Jones, Robert (Jesuit): Chirk.

Jones, Robert (writer): Llangynhafel.

Jones, Robert (VC): Raglan.

Jones, Sir Robert: Rhyl.

Jones, Robert (rugby): Trebanos.

Jones, Robert Ambrose (Emrys ap Iwan): Bodelwyddan.

Jones, Robert Gerallt: Nefyn.

Jones, Robert Meyrick (Bobi): Cardiff.

Jones, Robert Tudur: Llanystumdwy.

Jones, Robin: Gwytherin.

Jones, Roderick: Ferndale.

Jones, Rowland: Llanbedrog.

Jones, Sally Roberts: London.

Jones, Stephen: Rogerstone.

Jones, Steve: Tredegar.

Jones, Stuart Lloyd: Liverpool.

Jones, T. Gunstone: Pontarddulais.

Jones, T. Gwynn: Betws yn Rhos.

Jones, T. Harri: Llanafan Fawr.

Jones, Terry (actor): Colwyn Bay.

Jones, Terry (darts): Pontypridd.

Jones, Thomas (painter): Aberedw.

Jones, Thomas (scholar): Alltwen.

Jones, Thomas (hymnwriter): Caersws.

Jones, Thomas (missionary): Llangynyw.

Jones, Thomas (poet): Rhayader.

Jones, Thomas (educationist): Rhymney.

Jones, Thomas (Twm Siôn Catti): Tregaron.

Jones, Thomas (almanacker): Tre'r Ddol.

Jones, Sir Thomas: Pontnewydd.

Jones, Thomas Jarman: Llangristiolus.

Jones, Thomas Llewellyn (T. Llew): Pentrecwrt.

Jones, Thomas Owen: Pwllheli.

Jones, Thomas Robert: Llannefydd.

Jones, Tom (TUC): Rhosllanerchrugog.

Jones, Tom (singer): Treforest.

Jones, Tom Baker: Newport.

Jones, Trevor Stanley: Vaynor.

Jones, Tristan: Tristan da Cunha, South Atlantic.

Jones, Tudur Huws: Bangor.

Jones, W.E. (Willie): Carmarthen.

Jones, William (historian): Beddgelert.

Jones, Sir William: Calcutta, India.

Jones, William (mathematician): Llanfihangell Tre'r Beirdd.

Jones, William (eisteddfodwr): Llangadfan.

Jones, William Ellis: Abererch.

Jones, William Hughes: Rhyl.

Jones, William Samuel: Llanystumdwy.

Jones, William Tudur: Strata Florida.

Jones, Wyn: Llanrwst.

Jones-Parry, Sir Ernest: Rhuddlan.

Jones-Parry, Sir Love: Madryn.

Joseph, David: Swansea.

Joseph, Sir Leslie: Swansea.

Josephson, Brian: Cardiff.

Joshua, Lyn: Cardiff.

K

Kane, Vincent: Cardiff.

Karrie, Peter: Bridgend.

Keating, Joseph: Mountain Ash.

Keenor, Fred: Cardiff.

Kelsey, Jack: Llansamlet.

Kemble, Charles: Brecon.

Kern, Patricia: Swansea.

Kilvert, Francis: Hardenhuish, Hereford and Worcester.

King, Peter: Cardiff.

Kinney, Phyllis: Pontiac, USA.

Kinnock, Glenys: Roade, Northamptonshire.

Kinnock, Neil: Tredegar.

Knight, Bernard: Cardiff.

Krzywicki, Dick: Penley.

Kyffin, Maurice: Oswestry, Shropshire.

L

Labinsky, Alexander Numa (Count): Birmingham.

Lascelles, Arthur: Pennel.

Lavis, George: Sebastopol.

Lawrence, Syd: Shotton.

Lawrence, T.E. (Lawrence of Arabia): Tremadoc.

Leach, Arthur Leonard: Tenby.

Lefebre, Roland: Rotterdam, Netherlands.

Levi, Thomas: Ystradgynlais.

Lewes, William: Llwynderw.

Lewis of Caerleon: Caerleon.

Lewis, Allan: Pontypool.

Lewis, Alun: Cwmaman.

Lewis, Arthur: Crumlin.

Lewis, Ceri: Treorchy.

Lewis, David (martyr): Abergavenny.

Lewis, David (Jesus College): Abergavenny.

Lewis, David Vivian Penrose (Lord Brecon): Merthyr Tydfil.

Lewis, David Thomas: Brynmawr.
Lewis, Donna: Cardiff.
Lewis, Edward: Llangurig.
Lewis, Eiluned: Newtown.
Lewis, Francis: Newport.
Lewis, Geoff: Talgarth.
Lewis, Gwilym: Birmingham.
Lewis, Henry: Clydach.
Lewis, Sir Herbert: Mostyn.
Lewis, Howell Elvet (Elfed):
    Cynwyl Elfed.
Lewis, Hywel David: Waunfawr.
Lewis, Idris: Llansamlet.
Lewis, John: Old Radnor.
Lewis, John David: Llandyssul.
Lewis, Lewis Haydn: Aberaeron.
Lewis, Lewis William: Pensarn.
Lewis, Martyn: Swansea.
Lewis, Owen: Llangadwaladr.
Lewis, Richard (bishop): Henllan.
Lewis, Richard (tenor):
    Manchester.
Lewis, Richard (Dic Penderyn):
    Penderyn.
Lewis, Richard (Dick): Tonypandy.
Lewis, Robyn: Llangollen.
Lewis, Ronald: Port Talbot.
Lewis, Saunders: Wallasey, Cheshire.
Lewis, Sir Thomas: Cardiff.
Lewis, Tony: Swansea.
Lewis, William: Milford Haven.
Lewis, Sir Wilfred Hubert Poyer:
    London.
Lewis, William Robert:
    Llangristiolus.
Lewis, William Thomas (Lord
    Merthyr): Merthyr Tydfil.
Lewis, Sir Willmott Harsant:
    Cardiff.
Lewys Glyn Cothi: Llanybydder.
Lewys Morganwg (see Llywelyn
    ap Rhisart).
Lhuyd, Edward: Oswestry,
    Shropshire.

Lilly, Gwenith: Liverpool.
Lindsay, George Mackintosh:
    Cardiff.
Lindsay, Lionel: Brecon.
Linklater, Eric: Penarth.
Linton, John: Newport.
Livsey, Lord Richard: Troedyrhiw.
Livsey, Roger: Barry.
Llewellen, David:
    Haverfordwest.
Llewellyn, Carl: Pembroke.
Llewellyn, Sir David (journalist):
    Aberdare.
Llewellyn, Sir David (coalowner):
    Aberdare.
Llewellyn, Sir Godfrey: Bridgend.
Llewellyn, Gwyn: Bangor.
Llewellyn, Sir Harry: Merthyr
    Tydfil.
Llewellyn, Richard: St. David's
Llewellyn, William: Llantrisant.
Llewellyn, Willie: Tonypandy.
Llewellyn-Jones, Frederick:
    Bethesda.
Llewelyn, Desmond: Newport.
Lloyd, Charles: Llanfyllin.
Lloyd, D. Tecwyn: Glan-yr-afon.
Lloyd, David: Trelogan.
Lloyd, David Myrddin:
    Fforestfach.
Lloyd, Ellis: Newport.
Lloyd, Emmeline Lewis:
    Nantgwyllt.
Lloyd, Evan: Bala.
Lloyd, Henry: Llanbedr.
Lloyd, Illtyd Rhys: Port Talbot.
Lloyd, John (martyr): Brecon.
Lloyd, John (scholar): Brecon.
Lloyd, John (musician): Caerleon.
Lloyd, Sir John: Liverpool.
Lloyd, John (rugby): Pontycymmer.
Lloyd, John Ambrose: Mold.
Lloyd, John Morgan: Ton Pentre.
Lloyd, John Selwyn: Tal-y-sarn.

Lloyd, Robert (Llwyd o'r bryn): Cefnddwysarn.
Lloyd, Siân: Maesteg.
Lloyd, Tal: Merthyr Tydfil.
Lloyd, Thomas: Llanfyllin.
Lloyd, Thomas Alwyn: Liverpool.
Lloyd, Sir William: Wrexham.
Lloyd Jones, David Elwyn: Aberystwyth.
Llwyd, Alan: Dolgellau.
Llwyd, Angharad: Caerwys.
Llwyd, Elfyn: Betws-y-coed.
Llwyd (Lhuyd), Humphrey: Denbigh.
Llwyd, Morgan: Ffestiniog.
Llwyd, Richard (Bard of Snowdon): Beaumaris.
Llywelyn ap Rhisiart (Lewys Morganwg): Llantwit Major.
Llywellyn, Gareth: Cardiff.
Llywelyn, Robin: Llanfrothen.
Llywellyn-Davies, Lady Patricia: Bala.
Llywelyn-Williams, Alun: Cardiff.
Lodge, Diana: Tredegar.
Loosemore, Sarah: Cardiff.
Lord, Peter: Exeter, Devon.
Loveland, Kenneth: Sheerness, Kent.
Low, Andy Fairweather: Ystrad Mynach.
Lucas, Sir Charles Prestwood: Crickhowell.
Lush, Sir Archibald (Archie): Tredegar.
Lyne, Horace: Newport.
Lyne, Joseph Leycester (see Ignatius, Father).
Lynn-Thomas, Sir John: Llandyssul.

M

McConnon, Jim: Burnopfield, County Durham.
McDermid, Angus: Bangor.

Macdonald, Dick: Penley.
Macdonald, Gordon (Lord Macdonald of Gwaunysgor): Prestatyn.
Macdonald, Julien: Merthyr Tydfil.
MacDonald, Tom: Llandre.
McGrath, Michael Joseph: Kilkenny, Ireland.
Machen, Arthur: Caerleon.
Maddock, Ieuan: Gowerton.
Maddock, William Alexander: Fron Iw.
Maddocks, Ann: Llangynwyd.
Madoc, Philip: Merthyr Tydfil.
Madoc, Ruth: Norwich.
Madog ap Gwallter: Llanfihangel Glyn Myfyr.
Mahoney, Jack: Cardiff.
Mair, Angharad: Carmarthen.
Malcolm, Christian: Newport.
Manfield, Les: Mountain Ash.
Mansel, Bussy: Briton Ferry.
Mantle, John: Cardiff.
Mardy-Jones, Thomas Isaac: Brynaman.
Marks, Howard: Kenfig Hill.
Marquand, Richard: Cardiff.
Marshall, Walter (Lord): Cardiff.
Mars Jones, Sir William Lloyd: Llansannan.
Martin Allan: Port Talbot.
Mathias, John: Llanbadarn Fawr.
Mathias, Roland: Talybont-on-Usk.
Mathias, Ron: Pontarddulais.
Mathias, Tom: Cilgerran.
Mathias, William: Whitland.
Matthews, Abraham: Llanidloes.
Matthews, Cerys: Cardiff.
Matthews, Jack: Bridgend.
Matthews, Terry: Newbridge.
Maurice, Sir William: Dolbenmaen.
May, Phil: Llanelli.
Maynard, Matthew: Oldham, Lancashire.

Meade, Richard: Chepstow.
Medwin, Terry: Swansea.
Megane, Leila (see Hughes,
    Margaret).
Melhuish, Sir Charles: Cardiff.
Mercer, Jack: Southwick, Sussex.
Merchant, Moelwyn: Port Talbot.
Meredith, Billy: Chirk.
Meredith, Bryn: Pontnewynydd.
Meredith, Christopher: Tredegar.
Merrett, Sir Herbert: Cardiff.
Merrick, Rice: St Nicholas.
Merriman, John: London.
Michael, Alun: Colwyn Bay.
Michael, Glyndwr: Aberbargoed.
Michael, Jimmy: Aberaman.
Middleton, Sir Hugh: Denbigh.
Miles, Dillwyn: Newport (Pembs).
Miles, Gareth: Caernarfon.
Miles, John: Clifford, Hereford
    and Worcester.
Milland, Ray: Neath.
Millington, Arthur: Hawarden.
Mills, Richard: Llandeilo.
Millward, Edward (Ted): Cardiff.
Milnes-Walker, Nicolette: Cardiff.
Minhinnick, Robert: Neath.
Monaghan, Thomas: Abergavenny.
Mond, Alfred: Farnworth,
    Lancashire.
Money, Owen: Merthyr Tydfil.
Monger, Chris: Taffs Well.
Moon, Rupert: Birmingham.
Moore, Graham: Hengoed.
Moore, Sally: Cardiff.
Moore, Sean: Blackwood.
Morgan, Abel: Llanwenog.
Morgan, Cliff: Trebanog.
Morgan, Sir Clifford: Penygraig.
Morgan, David: Battle.
Morgan, David: Quakers Yard.
Morgan, David Rhys: Ammanford.
Morgan, Derec Llwyd:
    Cefnbrynbrain.

Morgan, Derek: Cardiff.
Morgan, Dyfnallt: Dowlais.
Morgan, Edward: Bettisfield.
Morgan, Elaine (singer): Cardiff.
Morgan, Elaine (writer):
    Pontypridd.
Morgan, Elena Puw: Corwen.
Morgan, Fay: Fishguard.
Morgan, George Osborne:
    Gothenburg, Sweden.
Morgan, Gerald: Brighton.
Morgan, Griffith (Guto Nyth
    Brân): Llanwonno.
Morgan, Gwyn: Aberdare.
Morgan, Harry: Goytre.
Morgan, Sir Henry: Cardiff.
Morgan, Hopkin: Tonteg.
Morgan, John (archbishop):
    Llandudno.
Morgan, John (poet): Llangelynin.
Morgan, John (industrialist):
    Llantwit Major.
Morgan, John (writer): Swansea.
Morgan, John Hartman:
    Ystradfellte.
Morgan, Julie: Dinas Powys.
Morgan, Kelly: Tonteg.
Morgan, Kenneth O.: London.
Morgan, Sir Morien: Bridgend.
Morgan, Prys: Cardiff.
Morgan, Rhodri: Cardiff.
Morgan, Rhys: Penrhiwceiber.
Morgan, Robert (poet): Aberdare.
Morgan, Robert (diver): Cardiff.
Morgan, Ted: Milford Haven.
Morgan, Teddy: Aber-nant.
Morgan, Sir Thomas (17th
    century soldier): Llangattock.
Morgan, Sir Thomas (16th
    century soldier): Pencarn.
Morgan, Tudur: Bangor.
Morgan, Thomas John: Glais.
Morgan, William (actuary):
    Bridgend.

Morgan, William (bishop):
Penmachno.
Moriarty, Paul: Morriston.
Moriarty, Richard: Gorseinon.
Morrell, Enoch: Troedyrhiw.
Morris, Alfred Edwin: Stourbridge,
Hereford and Worcester.
Morris, Lord Brian of Morris
Castle: Cardiff.
Morris, Sir Cedric: Swansea.
Morris, Charles: Oswestry,
Shropshire.
Morris, Edward: Cerrig-y-
drudion.
Morris, Hugh: Cardiff.
Morris, Jan: Clevedon, Somerset.
Morris, John: Llanfihangel Tre'r
Beirdd.
Morris, John: Talybont.
Morris, Johnny: Newport.
Morris, Kenneth Vennor:
Ammanford.
Morris, Sir Lewis: Carmarthen.
Morris, Lewis: Llanfihangel Tre'r
Beirdd.
Morris, Sir Rhys Hopkin: Caerau.
Morris, Richard: Llanfihangel
Tre'r Beirdd.
Morris, William (poet): Blaenau
Ffestiniog.
Morris, Willim: Llanfihangel Tre'r
Beirdd.
Morris, Wyn: Merthyr Tydfil.
Morris-Jones, Sir Henry: Waunfawr.
Morris-Jones, Huw: Mold.
Morris-Jones, Sir John: Trefor.
Morys, Huw: Llangollen.
Mostyn, Francis: Talacre.
Mouland, Mark: St Athan.
Mountjoy, Doug: Tir-y-berth.
Muncer, Len: London.
Murphy, Jimmy: Pentre.
Murphy, Paul: Usk.
Myrddin ap Dafydd: Mancot.

Myrddin-Evans, Sir Guilhaume:
Abertillery.

N

Narberth, John Harper:
Pembroke Dock.
Nash, David: Markham.
Nash, John: Cardigan.
Nash, Malcolm: Abergavenny.
Nash, Richard (Beau): Swansea.
Nash-Williams, Victor Earle:
Fleur-de-Llys.
Nation, Terry: Llandaff.
Nichol, Theodore: Llanelli.
Nichol, Williams: Haverfordwest.
Nicholas, James: St David's.
Nicholas, Jemima: Fishguard.
Nicholas, Peter: Newport.
Nicholas, Thomas Evan (Niclas y
Glais): Llanfrynach.
Nicholls, Sir David: Neath.
Nicholls, Gwyn: Westbury on
Severn, Gloucestershire.
Nicholson, Mavis: Briton Ferry.
Nisbet, Robert: Haverfordwest.
Noakes, George: Bwlch-llan.
Noble, Roy: Brynaman.
Norling, Clive: Neath.
Norris, Leslie: Merthyr Tydfil.
Norster, Robert: Ebbw Vale.
Nott, Sir William: Neath.
Novello, Ivor: Cardiff.
Nurse, Mel: Swansea.
Nuttall, Geoffrey: Colwyn Bay.

O

O'Brien, Sir Tom: Llanelli.
O'Callaghan, Eugene: Ebbw Vale.
O'Neill, Dennis: Pontarddulais.
O'Shea, Tessie: Cardiff.
O'Sullivan, Tyrone: Abercwmboi.
Ogmore, Lord (see Rees-
Williams, David Rees).
Ogwen, Jenny: Llandybie.

Ogwen, John: Bethesda.
Oliver, David Thomas: Cardiff.
Oldfield-Davies, Alun: Clydach.
Onions, Alfred: St George's, Shropshire.
Ontong, Rodney: Johannesburg, South Africa.
Ormond, John: Dunvant.
Orwig, Dafydd: Deiniolen.
Osmond, John: Abergavenny.
Owain Glyndŵr (Owain ap Gruffydd ap Madog): Sycharth.
Owain Lawgoch (Owain ap Thomas ap Rhodri): Tatsfield, Surrey.
Owain, Owain Llywellyn: Tal-y-sarn.
Owen, Alun: Menai bridge.
Owen, Arthur D.K.: Pontypool.
Owen, Bob (Croesor): Llanfrothen.
Owen, Dale: Merthyr Tydfil.
Owen, Daniel: Mold.
Owen, David (poet): Llanystumdwy.
Owen, David (Dafydd y Garreg Wen): Portmadog.
Owen, Dillwyn: Llanfairfechan.
Owen, Dyddgu: Pontrobert.
Owen, Edwin: Blaenau Ffestiniog.
Owen, Gareth: Cilfynydd.
Owen, George: Henllys.
Owen, Geraint Dyfnallt: Pontypridd.
Owen, Gerallt Lloyd: Sarnau.
Owen, Sir Goronwy: Aberystwyth.
Owen, Goronwy (poet): Llanfairmathafarn Eithaf.
Owen, Gwawr: Glynarthen.
Owen, Isambard: Chepstow.
Owen, Ivor John Caradoc (Baron Treowen): Llanarth.
Owen, Hugh: Denbigh.
Owen, Idloes: Merthyr Vale.
Owen, Sir Hugh: Llangeinwen.

Owen, Jamie: Pembroke Dock.
Owen, John (Owain Alaw): Chester, Cheshire.
Owen, Sir John: Dolbenmaen.
Owen, John Dyfnallt: Llangiwg.
Owen, Johnny: Merthyr Tydfil.
Owen, Mary: Llansawel.
Owen, Morfydd Llwyn: Treforest.
Owen, Owen: Machynlleth.
Owen, Richard Morgan (Dickie): Landore.
Owen, Robert: Newtown.
Owen, Thomas Arfon: Ystalyfera.
Owen, Wilfred: Oswestry, Shropshire.
Owen, Will: Blaina.
Owen, William (musician): Bangor.
Owen, William (dramatist): Carreg-cefn.
Owen, William (poet): Llangian.
Owen Pughe, William: Llanfihangel-y-pennant.
Owens, Philip: Wrexham.

P

Packer, Harry: Chipping Norton, Oxfordshire.
Padley, Walter: Chipping Norton, Oxfordshire.
Parfitt, Fred: Pontnewydd.
Page, Malcom: Knucklas.
Parker, Tom: Llansamlet.
Parkhouse, Gilbert: Swansea.
Parr-Davies, Harry: Briton Ferry.
Parry, Blanche: Bacton, Hereford and Worcester.
Parry, Dafydd: Rowen.
Parry, Sir David Hughes: Llanaelhaearn.
Parry, Gordon Samuel David (Lord Parry of Neyland): Neyland.
Parry, Gwenlyn: Deiniolen.
Parry, John (Bardd Alaw): Denbigh.

Parry, John (harpist): Nefyn.
Parry, John Orlando: London.
Parry, Joseph: Merthyr Tydfil.
Parry, Richard (Gwalchmai):
    Llanerch-y-medd.
Parry, Robert Williams: Tal-y-sarn.
Parry, Sarah Winifred: Welshpool.
Parry, Sir Thomas: Carmel.
Parry, William: Northop.
Parry, William J.: Bethesda.
Parry-Jones, David: Pontypridd.
Parry-Williams, Henry: Carmel.
Parry-Williams, Sir Thomas:
    Rhyd-ddu.
Pask, Alun: Blackwood.
Patti, Adelina: Madrid, Spain.
Paynter, Will: Whitchurch.
Pearce, David: Newport.
Pearson, Arthur: Pontypridd.
Pearson, Thomas William:
    Bombay, India.
Peate, Iorwerth: Llanbrynmair.
Peers, Donald: Ammanford.
Pendry, Gil: Swansea.
Pennant, Thomas: Whitford.
Penry, John: Llangammarch.
Perkins, John: Blaenavon.
Perrot, Sir John: Haroldston.
Peterson, Jack: Cardiff.
Petty, Gwyneth: Maesteg.
Philips, Sir John: Picton Castle.
Phillips, Dave: Wegburg, Germany.
Phillips, Edgar (Trefin): Tre-fin.
Phillips, Eluned (Luned Teifi):
    Cenarth.
Phillips, Glyn: Rhosllanerchrugog.
Phillips, Jane: Cardiff.
Phillips, Kevin: Hebron.
Phillips, Leighton: Briton Ferry.
Phillips, Morgan: Bargoed.
Phillips, Roland: St David's.
Phillips, Siân: Gwaun-Cae-
    Gurwen.
Phillips, Sir Thomas: Brynmawr.

Phillipps, Katherine (The
    Matchless Orina): London.
Philip, Peter: Cardiff.
Pickering, David: Briton Ferry.
Picton, Sir Thomas: Poyston.
Pierce, Thomas Jones: Liverpool.
Piper, Nicky: Cardiff.
Plummer, Reg: Newport.
Pode, Sir Edward Julian:
    Sheffield, South Yorkshire.
Pomeroy, Margaret: Treorchy.
Pleass, Jim: Cardiff.
Ponsonby, Sarah: Dublin, Ireland.
Powel, Robat: Tredegar.
Powel, Thomas: Llanwrtyd.
Powell, Annie: Llwynypia.
Powell, Dave: Dolgarrog.
Powell, David: Bryneglwys.
Powell, Dewi Watkin: Trecynon.
Powell, Felix: St Asaph.
Powell, Griffith James: Cardiff.
Powell, Ivor: Gilfach.
Powell, John: Wrexham.
Powell, Philip: Trallong.
Powell, Sir Ray: Pentre.
Powell, Rees (Rice): Jeffreyston.
Powell, Thomas: Monmouth.
Powell, Vavasor: Knucklas.
Powell, Wickham (Wick): Cardiff.
Powell, William (Wick): Aberbeeg.
Povey, Michael: Tremadoc.
Powys, John Cowper: Shirley,
    Derbyshire.
Preece, Sir William Henry:
    Bontnewydd.
Prendergast, Peter: Abertridwr.
Prescott, John: Prestatyn.
Presdee, Jim: Mumbles.
Price, Albert: Weare, Somerset.
Price, Berwyn: Tredegar.
Price, Brian: Deri.
Price, Charles: Pilleth.
Price, Gareth: Aberaeron.
Price, Graham: Moascar, Egypt.

Price, Sir John: Brecon.
Price, John: Neath.
Price, Margaret: Tredegar.
Price, Peter Owen: Swansea.
Price, Richard: Llangeinor.
Price, Robert: Cerrig-y-drudion.
Price, Terry: Hendy.
Price, Thomas (Carnhuanawc):
    Llanfihangel Bryn Pabuan.
Price, William: Rudry.
Price, William Geraint: Merthyr
    Tydfil.
Prichard, Caradog: Bethesda.
Pritchard, John: Llan-gan.
Pricharch, Marged: Tregaron.
Prichard, Matthew: Cheadle,
    Cheshire.
Prichard, Rhys (The Old Vicar):
    Llandovery.
Prichard, Thomas Jeffrey
    Llewelyn: Trallong.
Prichard, Thomas Owen: Pwllheli.
Priday, Alun: Cardiff.
Pritchard, Cliff: Pontypool.
Probert, Arthur: Aberaman.
Prosser, David: Cardiff.
Prosser, Idris Glyn: Glynneath.
Prosser, Ray: Pontypool.
Protheroe, Alun: Maesteg.
Pryce, Guto: Cardiff.
Pryce, Jonathan: Holywell.
Pryce, Thomas: Brymbo.
Pryce, Tom: Ruthin.
Pryce-Jones, Sir Pryce: Newtown.
Prydderch, Rees: Llandovery.
Prys, Edmwnd: Llanrwst.
Prys, Elis: Ysbyty Ifan.
Prys, Thomas: Denbigh.
Prys-Davies, Gwilym (Lord Prys-
    Davies of Llanegryn): Tywyn.
Prys-Jones, A.G.: Denbigh.
Puddicombe, Anne Adaliza
    Beynon: Newcastle Emlyn.
Pugh, Edward: Ruthin.

Pugh, Sir Idwal: Cowbridge.
Pugh, Jeremy: Builth Wells.
Pugh, Lewis Griffith Evans:
    Shrewsbury, Shropshire.

Q
Quinnell, Derek: Llanelli.
Quinnell, Scott: Llanelli.

R
Radcliffe, Charles: Merthyr Tydfil.
Radcliffe, Daniel: Treforest.
Radmilovic, Paulo: Cardiff.
Raine, Allan: Newcastle Emlyn.
Ratcliffe, Kevin: Mancroft.
Raybould, Bill: Cardiff.
Reardon, Ray: Tredegar.
Recorde, Robert: Tenby.
Reece, Gil: Cardiff.
Rees, Abraham: Llanbrynmair.
Rees, Angharad: Cardiff.
Rees, Arthur: Llangadog.
Rees, Brinley Roderick: Tondu.
Rees, Sir Beddoe: Maesteg.
Rees, Bowen: Llandybie.
Rees, Christopher: Bridgend.
Rees, Dai: Barry.
Rees, Daniel: Whitchurch-in-
    Cemais.
Rees, David Alwyn: Gorseinon.
Rees, Ebenezer: Sirhowy.
Rees, Elgan: Clydach.
Rees, Evan: Puncheston.
Rees, Garnet: Pontardawe.
Rees, Sir Goronwy: Aberystwyth.
Rees, Gwendolen: Aberdare.
Rees, Harry: Pontypridd.
Rees, Haydn: Gorseinon.
Rees, Hopkin: Cwmavon.
Rees, Hubert: Llangennech.
Rees, Hugh: Ammanford.
Rees, Ifor: Felinfoel.
Rees, Ioan Bowen: Dolgellau.
Rees, Sir James Frederick:
    Milford Haven.

Rees, John Frederick: Penuwch.
Rees, Leighton: Ynysybwl.
Rees, Linford: Burry Port.
Rees, Lionel: Caernarfon.
Rees, Mattie: Ammanford.
Rees, Merlyn (Lord Merlyn-
Rees): Cilfynydd.
Rees, Morgan John: Llanbradach.
Rees, Norman: Cardiff.
Rees, Robert Ithel Traherne:
Penarth.
Rees, Sarah Jane: Llangrannong.
Rees, Stephen: Ammanford.
Rees, Thomas Mardy: Skewen.
Rees, Thomas Wynford: Holyhead.
Rees, Roger: Aberystwyth.
Rees, Walter: Neath.
Rees, William: Aberyscir.
Rees, William (Gwilym
Hiraethog): Llansannan.
Rees-Williams, David Rees (Lord
Ogmore): Bridgend.
Regan, Robbie: Bargoed.
Reichel, Sir Harry: Belfast, Ireland.
Rendel, Stuart: Plymouth, Devon.
Reynolds, Oliver: Cardiff.
Rhigyfarch: Llanbadarn Fawr.
Rhydderch, Samantha Wynne:
Tenby.
Rhys Goch Eryri: Beddgelert.
Rhys, Edward Prosser: Bethel.
Rhys, Ernest: London.
Rhys, Gruff: Haverfordwest.
Rhys, Garel: Swansea.
Rhys, Sir John: Ponterwyd.
Rhys, Keidrych: Bethlehem.
Rhys, Matthew: Cardiff.
Rhys, Morgan: Cil-y-cwm.
Rhys-Williams, Sir Rhys: Miskin.
Rice, Anneka: Cowbridge.
Richard, Henry: Tregaron.
Richard, Ivor (Lord): Llanelli.
Richard, Timothy: Llandovery.
Richards, Alun: Pontypridd.

Richards, Brinley (Brynli): Maesteg.
Richards, Brinley: Carmarthen.
Richards, Ceri: Dunvant.
Richards, David: Cwmgwrach.
Richards, Elfyn John: Barry.
Richards, Maurice: Ystrad
Rhondda.
Richards, Melville: Llandeilo.
Richards, Rex: Newport.
Richards, Thomas (journalist):
Dolgellau.
Richards, Thomas (historian):
Talybont.
Richards, Thomas (playwright):
Tywyn.
Richards, Tom (journalist):
Dolgellau.
Richards, Tom (athlete): Risca.
Richards, Viv: Antigua, West
Indies.
Richards, William Leslie: Capel
Isaac.
Richardson, Dick: Newport.
Riches, Norman: Cardiff.
Ring, Mark: Cardiff.
Risman, Gus: Cardiff.
Robbins, Russell: Pontypridd.
Robbins, Ted: Wrexham.
Roberts, Bartholemew (Black
Bart): Little Newcastle.
Roberts, Ben: Bangor.
Roberts, Bryn: Abertillery.
Roberts, Brynley Francis: Aberdare.
Roberts, Dafydd: Aberystwyth.
Roberts, Dave: Southampton,
Hampshire.
Roberts, David (Telynor
Mawddwy): Llan-ym-
mawddwy.
Roberts, Eigra Lewis: Blaenau
Ffestiniog.
Roberts, Eleazer: Pwllheli.
Roberts, Emrys: Liverpool.
Roberts, Emrys Owen: Caernarfon.

Roberts, Evan: Loughor.
Roberts, Sir George: Aberystwyth.
Roberts, George: Mochdre.
Roberts, Glyn: Bangor.
Roberts, Gwilym: Cardiff.
Roberts, Gwyndaf: Bangor.
Roberts, Guto: Criccieth.
Roberts, Howell: Llangernyw.
Roberts, Huw: Bangor.
Roberts, John (Ieuan Gwyllt):
  Aberystwyth.
Roberts, John (rugby): Liverpool.
Roberts, John (billiards):
  Manchester.
Roberts, John (martyr):
  Trawsfynydd.
Roberts, Iwan: Carmarthen.
Roberts, Kate: Rhosgadfan.
Roberts, Lewis: Beaumaris.
Roberts, Lynette: Buenos Aires,
  Argentina.
Roberts, Meirion:
  Abergwyngregyn.
Roberts, Michael: Neath.
Roberts, Peter: Ferryside.
Roberts, Rachel: Aberystwyth.
Roberts, Richard: Llanymynych.
Roberts, Richard Gwylfa:
  Penmaenmawr.
Roberts, Robert (singer): Bala.
Roberts, Robert (Silyn): Llanllyfni.
Roberts, Robert Evan: Llanilar.
Roberts, Samuel (S.R.):
  Llanbrynmair.
Roberts, Selyf: Corwen.
Roberts, Thomas: Abererch.
Roberts, Thomas Francis:
  Aberdovey.
Roberts, Thomas Sumerville:
  Ruabon.
Roberts, Will: Ruabon.
Roberts, Wyn (Lord): Conwy.
Robinson, Steve: Cardiff.
Roddick, Winston: Caernarfon.

Roderick, John (Siôn Rhydderch):
  Cemais.
Rodrigues, Peter: Cardiff.
Rogers, Allan: Gelligaer.
Rogers, Handel: Llanelli.
Rolant, Lilio: Cardiff.
Rolls, Charles: Llangattock Vibon
  Abel.
Roos, William: Amlwch.
Rosser, Sir Melvyn: Swansea.
Rowe-Beddoe, David: Cardiff.
Rowland, Daniel: Nantcwnlle.
Rowland, Henry: Mellteyrn.
Rowland, Hugh: Llanrug.
Rowland, Sir John: Tregaron.
Rowland, Keith: Brithdir.
Rowland, Robert John:
  Abergwyngregyn.
Rowlands, Sir Archibald:
  Lavernock.
Rowlands, Dafydd: Pontardawe.
Rowlands, Ceinwen: Holyhead.
Rowlands, Clive: Cwmtwrch.
Rowlands, Euros: Carmarthen.
Rowlands, Henry: Llanidan.
Rowlands, Jane Helen: Menai
  Bridge.
Rowlands, John: Trawsfynydd.
Rowlands, Ken: Ynysybwl.
Rowlands, Robert Hugh: Tywyn.
Rowlands, Ted: Porthcawl.
Rubens, Bernice: Cardiff.
Rubens, Harold: Cardiff.
Ruddock, Gilbert: Cardiff.
Rush, Ian: St Asaph.
Russell, Earl Bertrand: Trelleck.
Russell, John: Holyhead.
Russell, Moses: Tredegar.

S
Salesbury, William: Llansannan.
Salter Davies, Emrys:
  Haverfordwest.
Salusbury, Thomas (plotter):
  Denbigh.

Salusbury, Thomas (poet): Chirk.
Samuel, Wynne: Ystalyfera.
Samwell, David: Nantglyn.
Saunders, Dean: Swansea.
Saunders, Erasmus: Clydney.
Sayce, George Ethelbert: Llangua.
Seager, John Elliot: Cardiff.
Seager, Sir William: Cardiff.
Secombe, Sir Harry: Swansea.
Shankland, Thomas: St Clears.
Shaw, Glyn: Rhigos.
Shaw, Ian: St Asaph.
Sheen, Jack: Aberdare.
Sheen, Michael: Newport.
Shepherd, Don: Port Eynon.
Sherman, Abe: Cardiff.
Sherman, Harry: Cardiff.
Sherwood, Alf: Cardiff.
Shields, Roberts: Cardiff.
Short, Charlie: Merthyr Tydfil.
Siddons, Sarah: Brecon.
Siemens, Sir William: Lenthe,
    Germany.
Simon, Robin John Hughes:
    Llandaff.
Sinnott, Kevin Fergus: Sarn.
Sion, Tudur: St Asaph.
Skaife, Sir Eric Ommaney:
    Chichester, Sussex.
Skrimshire, Reg: Crickhowell.
Slatter, Neil: Cardiff.
Smart, Cyril: Lacock, Wiltshire.
Smith, David (Dai): Tonypandy.
Smith, Sir James: Llandyssul.
Smith, Llew: Newbridge.
Smith, Patricia: Church Village.
Smith, Ray: Trealaw.
Smith, William Henry (Bill):
    Cardiff.
Smith, Sir William Reardon:
    Appledore, Devon.
Smithson, Florence: Merthyr Tydfil.
Soulsby, Sir Llewellyn Thomas
    Gordon: Swansea.

Southall, Neville: Llandudno.
Speed, Gary: Hawarden.
Spinetti, Victor: Cwm.
Sparke, Gareth: Swansea.
Squire, Jeff: Pontywaun.
Squire, William: Neath.
Squires, Dorothy: Pontyberem.
Stanley, Lady Dorothy:
    Cadoxton-juxta-Neath.
Stanley, Sir Henry Morton (John
    Rowlands): Denbigh.
Stanton, Charles Butt: Aberaman.
Stapledon, Sir George: Northam,
    Devon.
Stead, Peter: Barry.
Steer, Irene: Cardiff.
Stennett, Stan: Cardiff.
Stephen, Douglas Clark:
    Leicester, Leicestershire.
Stephens, Edward (Tanymarian):
    Ffestiniog.
Stephens, Emlyn: Cwmavon.
Stephens, Glyn: Neath.
Stephens, Ian: Tongwynlais.
Stephens, Meic: Treforest.
Stephens, Rees: Neath.
Stephens, Thomas (musician):
    Brynaman.
Stephens, Thomas (critic): Pont
    Neath Vaughan.
Stevens, Arthur Edwin:
    Monmouth.
Stevens, Mike: Solva.
Stevens, Shakin' (Michael
    Barrett): Cardiff.
Stone, Darwell: Rossett.
Stone, Jason: Cardiff.
Stonelake, Edward William:
    Pontlottyn.
Stradling, Sir Edward: St Donats.
Stringer, Howard: Cardiff.
Sulien (The Wise): Llanbadarn
    Fawr.
Sullivan, Jim: Cardiff.

Sutherland, Eric: Ammanford.
Sutton, Sir Graham: Cwmcarn.
Swain, Neil: Pontypridd.
Swann, Donald: Llanelli.
Symons, Arthur William: Milford Haven.

T

Taliesin: 'The Old North'.
Tamplin, Bill: Risca.
Tanner, Haydn: Gowerton.
Tapper-Jones, Sydney: Pentre.
Tapscott, Derick: Barry.
Taten, William James: Appledore, Devon.
Taylor, John: London.
Teale, Owen: North Cornelly.
Tear, Robert: Barry.
Temple-Morris, Peter: Penarth.
Templeton, Alec: Cardiff.
Terfel, Bryn: Penygroes.
Thomas, Sir Alfred (Lord Pontypridd): Cardiff.
Thomas, Aneurin: Ystalyfera.
Thomas, Sir Ben Bowen: Ystrad Rhondda.
Thomas, Bertie Pardoe: Newport.
Thomas, Brian: Neath.
Thomas, Brinley: Pontrhydyfen.
Thomas, Clem: Cardiff.
Thomas, Clive: Treorchy.
Thomas, Craig: Cardiff.
Thomas, Sir Daniel Lleufer: Cwmdu.
Thomas, Darren (snooker): Cwmfelinfach.
Thomas, Darren (cricket): Morriston.
Thomas, David (geographer): Bridgend.
Thomas, David (industrialist): Cadoxton-juxta-Neath.
Thomas, David (journalist): Cwmbran.

Thomas, David (WEA): Llanfechain.
Thomas, David Alfred (Lord Rhondda): Aberdare.
Thomas, David Vaughan: Ystalyfera.
Thomas, Delme: Bancyfelin.
Thomas, Dewi-Prys: Liverpool.
Thomas, Dylan: Swansea.
Thomas, Ebenezer: Llanarmon.
Thomas, Eddie: Merthyr Tydfil.
Thomas, Edward: London.
Thomas, Eric: Newport.
Thomas, Evan: Aber-porth.
Thomas, Frances: Aberdare.
Thomas, Frederick Jennings: Wenvoe.
Thomas, George (Lord Tonypandy): Port Talbot.
Thomas, Gethyn Stoodley: Pontypridd.
Thomas, Greg: Trebanos.
Thomas, Gwyn (novelist): Cymer.
Thomas, Gwyn (poet): Tanygrisiau.
Thomas, Hugh Hamshaw: Wrexham.
Thomas, Hugh Owen: Bodedern.
Thomas, Ifor: Glanaman.
Thomas, Ifor Owen: Traeth Goch.
Thomas, Ifor Rees: Bow Street.
Thomas, Sir Illtyd: Cardiff.
Thomas, Iorwerth: Clydach Vale.
Thomas, Sir Ivor B.: Dinas Powys.
Thomas, Ivor Owen: Briton Ferry.
Thomas, Iwan: Farnham, Surrey.
Thomas, J.B.G. (Bryn): Pontypridd.
Thomas, J.G. Parry: Wrexham.
Thomas, Jacob: Llanwinio.
Thomas, James Henry (Jimmy): Newport.
Thomas, James Purdon Lewis: Llandeilo.
Thomas, Jeffrey: Abertillery.
Thomas, John (Pencerdd Gwalia): Bridgend.

Thomas, John (photographer): Cellan.

Thomas, John (Ieuan Ddu): Carmarthen.

Thomas, John (Siôn o Eifion): Chwilog.

Thomas, John (songwriter): Newport.

Thomas, John (Eifionydd): Penmorfa.

Thomas, John Evan: Brecon.

Thomas, Sir John Meurig: Llanelli.

Thomas, John Prescott: Prestatyn.

Thomas, Joseph Anthony Charles: Bridgend.

Thomas, Kathleen: Penarth.

Thomas, Lewis: Llanfihangel Genau'r Glyn.

Thomas, Leslie: Newport.

Thomas, Louise Myfanwy: Holywell.

Thomas, Malcolm: Machen.

Thomas, Mansel: Tylorstown.

Thomas, Martin: Wrexham.

Thomas, Mary: Swansea.

Thomas, Melbourne: Newport.

Thomas, Mickey: Mochdre.

Thomas, Miles (Lord): Ruabon.

Thomas, Ned: Little Lever, Lancashire.

Thomas, Neil Roderick: Chirk.

Thomas, Pat: St Kitts, West Indies.

Thomas, Patrick: Welshpool.

Thomas, Sir Percy: South Shields, County Durham.

Thomas, Peter: Edinburgh.

Thomas, Peter (Lord Thomas of Gwydir): Llanrwst.

Thomas, R.S.: Cardiff.

Thomas, Rachel: Alltwen.

Thomas, Rhodri: Llanelli.

Thomas, Robert: Cwmparc.

Thomas, Robert Jermain: Abergavenny.

Thomas, Robert (ap Fychan): Llanuwchllyn.

Thomas, Richard: Trefeglwys.

Thomas, Rod: Glyncorrwg.

Thomas, Sir Roger: Cluderwen.

Thomas, Sidney Gilchrist: London.

Thomas, Simon: Lampeter.

Thomas, Stanley: Edinburgh, Scotland.

Thomas, Thomas (harpist): Bridgend.

Thomas, Thomas (Baptist): Cowbridge.

Thomas, Thomas Hendy: Pontypool.

Thomas, Thomas Llewelyn: Caernarfon.

Thomas, Tom: Penygraig.

Thomas, Trevor: Ynysddu.

Thomas, Sir Tudor: Ystradgynlais.

Thomas, William (Islwyn): Ynysddu.

Thomas, Sir William James: Caerphilly.

Thompson, David: London.

Thorburn, Paul: Rheindahl, Germany.

Thrale, Hestor: Nefyn.

Tilney, Harold: Newport.

Tilsley, Gwilym Richard (Tilsli): Llanidloes.

Tinker, David: London.

Titley, Mark: Swansea.

Tomkins, Thomas II: St David's.

Tomos, Angharad: Bangor.

Toshack, John: Cardiff.

Travers, George: Newport.

Travers, William (Bunner): Newport.

Treharne, Bryceson: Merthyr Tydfil.

Tress, David: London.

Trevithick, Richard: Illogan, Cornwall.

Trew, William John: Swansea.

Tripp, John: Bargoed.

Trow, Albert Howard: Newtown.
Trubshaw, Dame Gwendoline
   Joyce: Felinfoel.
Tucker, James: Cardiff.
Tucker, Norman: Swansea.
Tudor, Johnny: Mountain Ash.
Tudor, Richard: Llandrindod Wells.
Tudor Evans, Sir Haydn: Cardiff.
Tudur, Aled: Llansannan.
Turnbull, Maurice: Cardiff.
Turnbull, Bertrand: Cardiff.
Turner, John: Cardiff.
Tunnicliffe, Charles: Macclesfield,
   Cheshire.
Twiston-Davies, William
   Anthony: Monmouth.
Tyler, Bonnie: Skewen.

U

Ungoed-Thomas, Sir Lynn:
   Carmarthen.
Uzzell, John: Deri.

V

Valentine, Lewis: Llandulas.
Vaughan, Aled: Glyndyfrdwy.
Vaughan, Elizabeth: Llanfyllin.
Vaughan, Henry: Llansantffraid.
Vaughan, Hilda: Builth Wells.
Vaughan, John: Derllys Court.
Vaughan, Malcolm: Merthyr Tydfil.
Vaughan, Thomas: Llansantffraid.
Vaughan, William: Golden Grove.
Vaughan, William Herbert:
   Rogerstone.
Vaughan-Thomas, Wynford:
   Swansea.
Vernon, Roy: Ffynnongroew.
Vicari, Andrew: Port Talbot.
Vickery, Frank: Blaencwm.
Vile, Tommy: Newport.
Vivian, Henry Hussey (Baron
   Swansea): Swansea.

Vorderman, Carol: Prestatyn.
Vulliamy, Colwyn Edward:
   Glasbury.

W

Wade, Kirsty: Girvan, Scotland.
Wade-Evans, Arthur: Fishguard.
Wain, Richard: Penarth.
Walker, Nigel: Cardiff.
Walker, Peter: Bristol.
Wallace, Alfred: Llanbadon.
Walter, Lucy: Roch Castle.
Walters, Evan John: Llangyfelach.
Walters, Cyril: Bedlinog.
Walters, Gwynne: Gowerton.
Walters, Ivor: Chepstow.
Walters, John: Llanedi.
Walters, Thomas Glyn (Walter
   Glynne): Gowerton.
Walwyn, Fulke: Wrexham.
Warburton-Lee, Bernard: Maelor.
Ward, Donald: Trealaw.
Ward, John Aloysius: Leeds, West
   Yorkshire.
Waring, Anna Laetitia: Neath.
Waring, William: Welshpool.
Warner, John: Trealaw.
Warren, Huw: Swansea.
Watkin, Steve: Dyffryn Rhondda.
Watkins, Allan: Usk.
Watkins, David: Blaina.
Watkins, Mike: Abercarn.
Watkins, Morgan: Clydach.
Watkins, Sir Percy: Llanfyllin.
Watkins, Stuart: Newport.
Watkins, Sir Tasker: Nelson.
Watkins, Tudor (Baron
   Glyntawe): Abercraf.
Watkins, Vernon: Maesteg.
Watts, Helen: Milford Haven.
Watts, William: Chipping
   Sodbury, Gloucestershire.
Watts-Morgan, David (Dai): Neath.
Wayne, Naunton: Llanwonno.

Weale, Henry: Shotton.
Webb, Harri: Swansea.
Webber, Sir Robert John: Barry.
Webbe, Glyn: Cardiff.
Webster, Colin: Cardiff.
Webster, J. Roger: Caerwen.
Webster, Richard: Swansea.
Weekes, Philip: Tredegar.
Wells, Gordon: Porth.
Wells, Nigel: Northampton.
Welsh, Freddie (Frederick Hall Thomas): Pontypridd.
Westlake, Clive: Wattsville.
Weston, Simon: Nelson.
Wheatley, Ossie: Gateshead, County Durham.
Wheel, Geoff: Swansea.
Wheeler, Dame Olive Annie: Brecon.
Wheldon, Sir Huw: Bangor.
Wheldon, Sir Wyn Powell: Ffestiniog.
Whittaker, Tom: Porthmadog.
Whittington, Thomas Aubrey Leyshon (Tal): Neath.
White, Eirene (Baroness): Belfast.
White, Rawlins: Cardiff.
Whitefoot, Jeff: Bedwas.
Whitehouse, Paul: Ferndale.
Wilde, Jimmy: Quakers Yard.
Wilkins, Alan: Cardiff.
Wilkins, Frederick James: Cardiff.
Wilkinson, John: Clifton, Cumbria.
Wigley, Dafydd: Caernarfon.
William, Thomas (hymnwriter): Pendoylan.
William, Thomas (scientist): Swansea.
Williams, Alan: Caerphilly.
Williams, Alice Matilda Langland: Oystermouth.
Williams, Alun: Swansea.
Williams, Alwyn: Aberdare.
Williams, Ann: Rosemarket.

Williams, Arthur J.: Coychurch.
Williams, Bleddyn: Taffs Well.
Williams, Bryn: Pontypridd.
Williams, Brynmor: Cardigan.
Williams, Chrles (Lord Williams of Elvet): Llansantffraid.
Williams, Sir Charles Hanbury: Pontypool.
Williams, Clive: Porthcawl.
Williams, Daniel Howell: Ffestiniog.
Williams, Daniel Powell (Pastor Dan): Penygroes.
Williams, David (football): Cwmparc.
Williams, David (minister): Llanwrtyd.
Williams, David (historian): Llanycefn.
Williams, David (MP): Swansea.
Williams, David Glyndwr Tudor: Carmarthen.
Williams, David John (author): Corris.
Williams, David John (nationalist): Rhydycymerau.
Williams, Dennis: Aberaman.
Williams, Denzil: Trefil.
Williams, Edward: Eglwysilan.
Williams, Edward (Iolo Morganwg): Penmon.
Williams, Eliseus (Eifion Wyn): Porthmadog.
Williams, Elwyn William: Llangefni.
Williams, Emlyn (miners): Aberdare.
Williams, Emlyn (actor): Mostyn.
Williams, Evan: Cowbridge.
Williams, Evan: Maesteg.
Williams, Sir Evan: Pontarddulais.
Williams, Freddie: Port Talbot.
Williams, Gareth (historian): Barry.

Williams, Gareth (rugby): Bedlinog.
Williams, Gareth Howel:
Treherbert.
Williams, Gareth Wyn (Lord
Williams of Mostyn): Prestatyn.
Williams, George: Haverfordwest.
Williams, Gerwyn: Glyncorrwg.
Williams, Sir Glanmor: Dowlais.
Williams, Glanville Llewellyn:
Bridgend.
Williams, Glyn: Glyncorwg.
Williams, Grace: Barry.
Williams, Griffith John: Cellan.
Williams, Griffith P.: Llithfaen.
Williams, Gwilym: Aberdare.
Williams, Gwilym Owen:
Llanberis.
Williams, Gwyn (poet): Port Talbot.
Williams, Gwyn (rugby): Taffs Well.
Williams, Gwyn A.: Dowlais.
Williams, Herbert: Aberystwyth.
Williams, Hugh: Machynlleth.
Williams, Huw Owen (Huw
Menai): Caernarfon.
Williams, Huw Tregelles:
Gowerton.
Williams, Sir Ifor: Tregarth.
Williams, Iolo Aneurin:
Middlesborough, Cleveland.
Williams, Iris: Pontypridd.
Williams, Isaac: Llangorwen.
Williams, Islwyn: Ystalyfera.
Williams, J.E. Carwyn: Ystalyfera.
Williams, J.J.: Nantyffyllon.
Williams, J.P.R.: Cardiff.
Williams, James: Llansadwrn.
Williams, John (VC 1879):
Abergavenny.
Williams, John (archbishop):
Conwy.
Williams, John (VC 1918):
Nantyglo.
Williams, John (snooker):
Wrexham.

Williams, John (educationist):
Ystrad Meurig.
Williams, John (ap Ithel): Tynant.
Williams, Sir John: Gwynfe.
Williams, John Ellis Caerwyn:
Gwaun-Cae-Gurwen.
Williams, John G.: Llangwnadl.
Williams, John George: Cardiff.
Williams, John James (J.J.):
Talybont.
Williams, John Lewis: Aber-arth.
Williams, John Owen (Pedrog):
Madryn.
Williams, John Robert: Llangybi.
Williams, John Stuart: Mountain
Ash.
Williams, Johnny: Barmouth.
Williams, Sir Kyffin: Llangefni.
Williams, Leonard David: London.
Williams, Les: Trimsaran.
Williams, Llewellyn William:
Llanddeusant.
Williams, Lloyd: Taffs Well.
Williams, Llywelyn: Llanelli.
Williams, Margaret Lindsay: Barry.
Williams, Maria Jane:
Aberpergwm.
Williams, Mark: Cwm.
Williams, Miles: St Fagans.
Williams, Moses: Cellan.
Williams, Penry: Merthyr Tydfil.
Williams, Peter (rugby): Cwmparc.
Williams, Peter (hymnwriter):
Laugharne.
Williams, Phil: Bargoed.
Williams, Raymond: Pandy.
Williams, Rhodri: Cardiff.
Williams, Rhydwen: Pentre.
Williams, Rhys: Cwmllynfell.
Williams, Rhys Watcyn: Caerleon.
Williams, Richard Bryn: Blaenau
Ffestiniog.
Williams, Richard Tecwyn:
Abertillery.

Williams, Robert (Trebor Mai): Llanrhychwyn.

Williams, Robert Hugh: Bala.

Williams, Robert John (Prysor): Trawsfynydd.

Williams, Robert (Robert ap Gwilym Ddu): Llanystumdwy.

Williams, Sir Roger: Penrhos.

Williams, Rowland (Hwfa Môn): Trefdraeth.

Williams, Samuel Edward: Mancot.

Williams, Stephen J.: Ystradgynlais.

Williams, Stewart: Cardiff.

Williams, T. Arfon: Treherbert.

Williams, Taliesin: Cardiff.

Williams, Thomas (Tom Nefyn): Bodfuan.

Williams, Sir Thomas: Aberdare.

Williams, Thomas Eifion Hopkins: Cwmtwrch.

Williams, Thomas Rhondda: Cowbridge.

Williams, Waldo: Haverfordwest.

Williams, W.S. Gwyn Williams: Llangollen.

Williams, William (VC): Amlwch.

Williams, William (Crwys): Craigcefnparc.

Williams, William (Creuddynfab): Creuddyn.

Williams, William (o'r Wern): Llanfachreth.

Williams, William (Pantycelyn): Llandovery.

Williams, Sir William: Nantanog.

Williams, William (vet): St Asaph.

Williams, William John: Swansea.

Williams, Zephaniah: Bedwellty.

Williams-Ellis, Sir Clough: Gayton, Northamptonshire.

Williamson, Edward William: Cardiff.

Willis, Albert Charles: Tonyrefail.

Willis, Rex: Ystrad Rhondda.

Willows, Ernest Thompson: Cardiff.

Wilson, Cliff: Tredegar.

Wilson, David: Edinburgh, Scotland.

Wilson, Richard: Penygoes.

Windsor, Bobbie: Newport.

Winfield, Bert: Nottingham, Nottinghamshire.

Wingfield, Walter: Llanelidan.

Winstone, Howard: Merthyr Tydfil.

Wire, Nicky: Blackwood.

Woodroffe, Maurice: Cardiff.

Wooller, Wilfred: Rhos-on-Sea.

Woosnam, Ian: Oswestry, Shropshire.

Wright, Sir Charles: Birmingham.

Wroth, William: Abergavenny.

Wyatt, Mark: Crickhowell.

Wynn, Sir John: Gwydir.

Wynne, David: Hirwaun.

Wynne, Edith: Northop.

Wynne, Ellis: Harlech.

Y

Yale, Elihu: Boston, USA.

Yorath, Terry: Cardiff.

Yorke, Philip: Erddig.

Young, David: Aberdare.

Young, Eric: Singapore.

Young, James Jubilee: Maenclochog.

Young, Jeff: Blaenavon.

Young, Thomas: Hodgeston.

Z

Zimmern, Sir Alfred: Surbiton, Surrey.

Zobole, Ernest: Ystrad Rhondda.

NOTES

NOTES

NOTES

NOTES

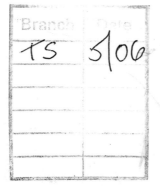